About Daniel Masias

1. He has the same birthdate as John Paul II - May 18th.

2. In the star cluster of Orion, there is a star named Meissa that is related to his name. His son's middle name is Ryan in honor of Orion.

3. May 18 is considered, by the Chinese, to be a lucky day to marry. Asia is also in his last name: Masias.

4. In the 1890's, Percival Lowell, in Flagstaff, Arizona, named a spot on Martian maps for Daniel's last name: Thau Masias

5. On December 23, 1993 a Jewish group from Israel announced that they were going to build a new temple to the Messiah, not far from Daniel's home.

6. On January 25, 2001 a new dinosaur was named The Masia Kasaurs. Daniel has a 100 ton granite dinosaur boulder on his property.

7. In July of 2012, geologists announced the new name of the super continent 100 million years in the future. It is named Amasia; Daniel A Masias' name.

8. Daniel's mother, Helen, went to the Great *Beyond* on April 20, 2014, Easter Sunday morning. This is the holiest day of Christianity. Without the rising of the Son, this religion is not legitimate.

The Man Who Walked Out of the Pages of History I

Daniel Masias

authorHOUSE®

AuthorHouse™
1663 Liberty Drive
Bloomington, IN 47403
www.authorhouse.com
Phone: 1 (800) 839-8640

Published by AuthorHouse 05/24/2017

ISBN: 978-1-5246-1107-1 (sc)
ISBN: 978-1-5246-1106-4 (e)

This book is dedicated to
Fawn, Somer, Jeff, Becky, Lilliana, Meriella

And to
Pythagorus, Aristotle, Plato, Socrates, Hippocrates,
Herodotus, Da Vinci, Michelangelo, Nostradamus, Galileo,
Tyco, Kepler, Guten- berg, Faraday, Clausius, Darwin,
Tesla, Einstein, and the millions of other enlightened
people of all the races of mankind throughout history.

This book is also dedicated to the hundreds of millions
of innocent human beings who were enslaved, tortured,
unjustly accused and murdered by Emperors, Kings,
Conquerors, Popes, Inquisitors, religious fanatics, dictators,
tyrants, despots, strong men, war chiefs, corrupt
governments and every manner of mantle
that evil men have used to
justify the killing of innocent men, women, children and
babies, throughout history....from all the races of mankind.

How Daniel Masias discovered highly advanced humanoid entities, who are visiting his archeology home site. These entities are probably billions of years old and are connected to our sun.

Daniel Masias - pronounced Messiah

Daniel's name is in this book

Source:

The Oxford English Dictionary, On The Origin of English Words. Copies of this scholarly book are in libraries and cities all over the world.

It is a universally accepted source of information.

-ACAL.] = MESSIANIC.
1614 JACKSON Creed III. xviii ..] ..for Propheticall, nor Apostolicall, nor Messiajall : much lesse could Papall authority make them bell ie/

Messiah (mɪˈsaɪə). Forms: α. 4 Messie, 4-5 Messye, 5 Messy, Messe, Myssye; β. 3 Messyas, 4-8 Messias; γ. 7 Messiab. [The α forms are a. F. Messie, ad. L. (Vulg.) Messiās, a. Gr. Μεσσίας, ad. Aramaic m'shīḥā, Heb. māshīaḥ anointed (in the LXX rendered Χριστός, CHRIST), f. māshaḥ to anoint. These forms do not occur in any Eng. transl. of the Bible, though common in other literature down to the 15th c. The form Messias was used in John i. 41 and iv. 25 (the only passages in which the word is found in the Gr. or Latin N.T.) by Wyclif after the Vulgate, and by later translators from 1526 to 1611 directly after the Greek. The form Messiah, invented by the translators of the Geneva Bible of 1560, is an alteration of the traditional Messias, intended to give it a more Hebraic aspect (the translators having on principle eliminated the Græcized forms of proper names from the O.T., though retaining them in the N.T.). In the Bible of 1611 it was adopted in Dan. ix. 25, 26, and although it occurs in no other passage of the 'Authorized Version', it eventually became the only current form. The Revisers of 1880-84 have substituted it for Messias in the two N.T. passages, but on the other hand have removed it from its original place in Dan. ix. where they read 'the anointed'.] The Hebrew title (= 'anointed') applied in the O.T. prophetic writings to a promised deliverer of the Jewish nation, and hence applied to Jesus of Nazareth as the fulfilment of that promise. (Chiefly preceded by the or defining word, exc. in the three Bible passages and sometimes in poetry, where it is treated as a proper name.) Hence transf., an expected liberator or saviour of an oppressed people or country. (Written with capital M.)

α. *1].. Propr. Sanct. (Vernon MS.) in Archiv Stud. neu. Spr. LXXXI. 87/152 Andrew ſenne to Symound tolde: 'Messye we ha founde'. ?a 1400 Morte Arth. 3998 Here I make myn avowe,..To Messie, and to Marie. 1430-40 LYDG. Bochas IX. i. 10 b, Sayd openly that he was Messy. c 1500 Cov. Corpus Chr. Plays I. 425 Yt ys seyd..That of the lyne of Jude Schuld spryng a right Messe.

messiah (n.)

c.1300, Messias, from Late Latin Messias, from Greek Messias, from Aramaic meshiha and Hebrew mashiah "the anointed" (of the Lord), from mashah "anoint." This is the word rendered in Septuagint as Greek Khristos (see Christ). In Old Testament prophetic writing, it was used of an ex- pected deliverer of the Jewish nation. The modern English form represents an attempt to make the word look more Hebrew, and dates from the Geneva Bible (1560). Transferred sense of "an expected liberator or savior of a captive people" is attested from 1660s.

http://www.etymonline.com/index.php?term=messiah

Accepted scientific statement by the Astro Scientists of the World

13.8 billion years ago, the Big Bang took place. This event created the most abundant element in the visible universe; hydrogen gas. This element, as well as, gravity led the creation of the stars and galaxies as we see them today. Since the creation of our solar system some 4.8 billion years ago, our solar system has made 18 revolutions around the center of our Milky Way Galaxy.

Contents

Chapter 1   LA JUNTA

The first person I saw when I came into this world was a young man from Japan. My mother called him Dr. Shima. The national flag of Japan is the rising sun. The rising sun set the stage for the rest of my life. It would be decades before I began to realize that my life was one mystery after another. I would figure it out.

It was May 18, 1949, the year that I was born. May 18 is the day that Pope John Paul II was born. The implications of this sacred Chinese Lucky Day have followed and protected me all the days of my life. Dr. Hiro Shima, a young Japanese Physician, helped bring me into this world at the local hospital, a sun-drenched farming community, of La Junta, Colorado. Doctor Shima was forced from his home in California, as well as, thousands of other Japanese-Americans, and placed in internment camps at the break of World War II. Dr. Shima came from a camp near La Junta. He must have liked the community because after the war he stayed on in the La Junta region. I don't know any history of Dr. Hiro Shima, except that my mother, Helen Masias, said he was a young and good doctor.

The Egyptians, Greeks and Romans all said that we are given our fates. After experiencing all the strange events of my life, what Albert Einstein spoke about concerning the universe, and conducting my scientific investigations – I am thoroughly convinced that we are all given our fates before birth. Four decades after my birth I began to realize Dr. Shima was the first person, besides Helen, who would be a symbol of my fate. That would follow me all of my life. One day in 2008 a scientific epiphany would be revealed to me. This epiphany would be a very interesting scientific discovery based on Albert Einstein's E=MC2.

The Webster's Dictionary defines a patriarchal family as a social system in which the chief authority is the father or eldest male member of the family or clan. Dan Masias Sr., my father, perfectly matches the definition of a patriarchal supreme authority figure. From 1949 until around 1975 Dan Sr. had control over me, as well as all of his children. Patriarchal Clans are a common form of human existence found all over the world. Anthropology studies suggest that this phenomenon has existed for thousands of years and probably led to the banding together of like minded people for the purpose of survival. The banding together of these common heritage people then led to small villages and these villages led to small city states. Eventually, city states led to great civilizations and the modern world we live in today.

The earliest memory I have of myself is very strange. I am in a white hospital room and I am standing and looking at a young woman laying on a white hospital bed. Her shoulder-length dark hair is limp and sweaty and she is moving in the bed as she is experiencing the pain of child birth. A male figure dressed in a hospital gown and white cap is at the head of the bed, and is looking down on Helen, as she moans and groans in pain. I sense that this male figure is her protector. Through some sort of unknown extrasensory perception this white figure indicates to me that Helen is doing good in delivering me into the world on May 18, 1949. The figure I see hovering over Helen appears to be dressed in a white hospital gown and yet he also appears to be a somewhat ghostly figure. From my physical perspective, I am standing on Helen's right side facing the hospital bed and I am as tall as the white male figure! How can I be standing in a hospital room thinking and watching myself being born? The closer I look at the male figure over Helen I realize that I cannot make out any facial features. I am looking at the side of this very important entity.

In 1949, Dr. Hiro Shima is a young Japanese man and he should exhibit Asian facial features with short black hair. The mysterious person does not have black hair or Asian facial features. The figure that I am watching is made out of some sort of white plasma energy.

2

I can see the right side and front of his body and he is not a human being! The hospital room that I am in is not a hospital room. I cannot see a single hospital related item, such as tables, cabinets with glass doors, towels or medical instruments that would have been typical of a hospital birthing room in 1949. the room that I am in, with Helen and the energy figure is completely white; not a blinding white color but a soft white glow. Sixty years later, at my home and research site (where I saw two small Bigfoot creatures), my infrared night vision cameras have taken color photos, on a number of occasions, of a humanoid white plasma energy entity that looks like the white ghostly figure that is watching over Helen as she is giving birth to me!

The next memory that I have is of living in Otero County in Swink, Colorado between Rocky Ford and La Junta. I was about 3 years old. Dan, Helen, Patricia, Donald (as an infant) and I lived in a small cream colored wood sided home. The tiny home was located right next to busy highway 50. The railroad tracks and the Arkansas River were just north of our home. The River fed irrigation water to the entire region's farms and fields which grew watermelons, cantaloupes, beans, onions, sugar beets, etc. Our home was on the side of Highway 50 and there was a road on the left side of the property that went north. Parallel to the road, right next to our tiny home, was an irrigation ditch with about 18 to 24 inches of muddy brown water. The property where we lived had many large cottonwood trees on the north, east, south and west sides, starting at about 100 feet from the home. A small driveway with a culvert that directed the irrigation water past the house allowed automobiles access to the back of the home. I never saw a driveway in the front of the home with access to highway 50. Directly across the street, west of our tiny home, stood a larger much nicer home. This home faced highway 50 and had access through the front. The home had been converted to a grocery store.

I remember walking up the three or four steps to the front roof covered columned porch. A screen door then opened into the small country grocery store. The outside of this home store was painted a dark brown as opposed to our cream colored home. The whole area, from what I can remember, was a beautiful farming community. There were lush green planted fields south of our home across paved highway 50. The road parallel to the irrigation ditch was a country dirt road. Being a small 3 year old child I could see large beautiful cottonwood trees everywhere down the dirt road towards the Arkansas River and the train tracks. Cottonwoods are known to grow up around rivers or where there is abundant water sources. As a three year old boy I had a sense of appreciation for the physical beauty of the land. There were wildflowers and tall lush grass all over our yard and the neighborhood. I remember being happy.

On the property boundaries there was old rusty grid-wire fencing and parts of it were sagging and falling down. On the eastern section of the yard were a couple of old chicken coops. I remember going into these two small sheds. They were dark inside except for the streaks of sunlight shining through the long cracks on the outside walls. Inside there was chicken droppings everywhere and the smell of urine and ammonia. I can still, to this day, remember exploring those two chicken coops with trepidation. I was too afraid to go inside but once I did my fear disappeared. The ammonia and smell of chicken droppings was very strong. Helen had told me what the two sheds were. And as a small child, I asked where did the chickens go?" I was very sad. For some unexplained reason, at that moment, in my 3 year old life, I developed a great interest in events of the past. My love of history, archaeology and science grew as I became older. Science has now proven that chickens and birds are related to dinosaurs. In 1982, when I built my home on Hondo, my question as a three year old as to 'where did the chickens go' would be answered.

Profound events happened to me at the little rundown cream colored miniature ranch house. One day on a summer morning I was outside on the side of the road and near the irrigation ditch. Suddenly, out of nowhere, a giant pink pig came trotting past me at a distance of about 8 feet. I was petrified at the sight of this pig. At that time, I did not understand what a pig was or how dangerous a grown pig could be to a 3 year old. If the pig had attacked me I could have died right there. Abraham the great patriarch of the Jews, in the teachings of the Torah, forbid eating the meat of the unclean pig. Later in my life, genealogical research would reveal that I have a Jewish heritage. I believe that an unseen omnipotent force of good, because of my Jewish heritage, protected me from that 200 pound pig.

We must have lived at this tiny farm house for three years or so because I remember being a toddler about 13 months old. When the Masias family first moved into the little house I remember being outside on the driveway. I must have just learned to walk because I remember wearing a little white t shirt. There was a small little white dog in the driveway. I remember trying to walk fast with choppy little baby steps after the dog. My little arms outstretched and my baby hands were trying to coax the dog to come to me. I was fascinated with the cute dog and wanted to touch it. The dog was walking away from me, but it suddenly bolted around at me and jumped at my head. It bit me on the upper lip just below my nose. The dog attack was very frightful to me. From the growling sound of dog anger when it hit my little face to the intense physical pain as the canine teeth punctured my lip. As I got up off the ground I was in intense pain, confused and scared. Then I felt warm liquid flowing into my mouth and I looked down and saw bright red blood covering my little white shirt. All this time I am crying and in great pain. I was not taken to a doctor or hospital for medical treatment. To this day I am NOT positive what attacked me because I was so little and had just learned to walk. It could have been a small white cat, large white rat, small rabbit or a little white dog.

Patricia and I were outside in the backyard next to the irrigation ditch. It was a warm sunny summer day. We were playing and doing what a three and two year old girl would do; picking flowers, picking up rocks and sticks and kicking at things on the ground. Patricia was walking near me as she followed me where I went. We were near the gently flowing irrigation ditch when Patricia walked too close to the soft bank. She tumbled into the muddy water. Being only two years old, she was pretty tiny. She fell in completely from head to toe. She was screaming and then yelping because water was getting into her mouth. She was laying down flat in the water with her head facing the bottom of the ditch. She was trying to get up out of the water with her little hands and feet, but at 18 to 24 inches deep, the muddy sides and bottom of the ditch prevented her from getting out of the water. I immediately tried to pull her out of the water. Somehow, I got right to the edge of the ditch without it giving way and me falling into the water as well. I could not grab her left arm because she was panicked and moving back and forth. I was down on my hands and knees trying to grab her left hand or arm and pull her out. There was no way to reach this little girl without me falling into the water, as well. Then, by incredible good luck, I was able to grab her long black hair, floating in the water and drag her up and over the side of the flowing ditch water. I pulled her as hard as I could by her hair and was able to get her completely out of the water. If I had not had a sense of responsibility to this little kid sister or if I had panicked and ran off looking for Dan or Helen, Patricia would have drowned in that ditch. When I was finally able to get her out of the water, because I had trouble getting her completely out, she looked like a little wet rag doll. She collapsed to the ground and was crying after I got her out. At some point, Helen heard Patricia crying and came outside. I told her that Patricia fell into the water and I pulled her out by her hair.

Patricia Masias was born in La Junta, Colorado. Donald Masias was born in La Junta, Colorado. Glen Masias was born in La Junta. Timothy Masias was born in La Junta.

When I lived at the little cream colored house I have no memory of Donald, Glen or Timothy at all except for one very frightening event. One summer day in 1956 or 1957 when the Masias family lived in Pueblo, Dan and Helen took me, Pat, Don, Glen, Tim and Sam on a picnic to Holbrook Lake near La Junta. It was a blazing hot day and I would have been seven or eight years old. I remember walking with Dan and Helen and all these kids through trees and white sand next to the lake. I remember almost stepping on a broken Pepsi bottle with bare feet and cringing at what could have severely cut my foot open. I picked it up and put it in the trash. After a picnic of watermelon, Tim, Don or Glen and I got into the edge of the water about two feet deep. We were playing in the water and did not notice that Tim, who was two or three years old, was now beginning to drown in three to four feet deep water. I lunged forward and grabbed his little arm and shoulder and yelled "Dad!" I helped him up and Dan ran into the water in a panic and pulled him to shore. None of us knew how to swim.

Flashback

When I was about 13 months old I believe the Masias family moved into the small cream colored home. I believe that we lived there for one or two years. During this time I wandered outside by myself until Patricia was old enough to walk outside with me. I cannot remember supervision outside by Dan or Helen. I do remember walking over to the little grocery store with Patricia in tow. I remember how excited I was to go into the grocery store. I remember looking into the dark cherry wood cabinets and seeing many kinds of candy. I was very happy when Dan put four or five different boxes of Wrigley's chewing gum in front of me on the glass case top as I stood on a chair. I remember picking up brand new packs of gum and I could smell the wonderful chewing gum odor. I was very happy to visit that store. I was only 3 years old and crossing a dirt road to get to the grocery store. I wandered between our tiny home and the little grocery store on a regular basis.

After Helen saw that I had pulled Patricia from the irrigation ditch we still played outside. While living at this location next to the very busy Highway 50 an astonishing event happened on a beautiful bright sunny morning. Over the years I have given this event analytical thought and tried to determine the meaning of what I saw. On that morning, in the summer of 1953, I was outside at the back of the house on the driveway and I was playing. I loved the big cottonwood trees that were on the property. I must have seen a shiny reflection of light above the top of the trees because I looked up to the top of the trees. I was facing north of the back of the property and parallel to the dirt road and irrigation ditch. In the distance, about 100 feet or so away, and just above the tree top canopy, a bright silvery disk or cigar shaped UFO object was silently hovering in the morning sunshine. I was 3 or 3 ½ years old I did not know what I was looking at. I can clearly see the objects curved sides and what appeared to be three or four square windows. I cannot be positive, but I may have seen several dark humanoid figures staring back at me from inside this flying aircraft.. This event must have happened about 11 a.m. or so because of the angle of the sun's rays on the hovering object. As I have thought about my encounter with this UFO, as a small child - this event, as well as my experience of watching myself being born - set the stage and theme for the rest of my life. At the time, I did not realize the importance of these events to my life until I built my home on Hondo.

After my sighting of the UFO, at the little tiny home next to highway 50, Dan and Helen moved us to a small home in Rocky Ford Colorado. I was three or three and a half when we moved to a small home. To this day, I do not know where in Rocky Ford this home was located, unlike our previous house next to highway 50. The best time that I have figured, is that this new home may have been located near Dan's parents' home, whom I knew as Jocobh and George. Rocky Ford in 1953 - 1954 was a tiny farming community with highway 50 running through the middle of town. I remember there were several new and used car dealerships located on highway 50 right in the center of town. They ran from east to west on the south side of the highway. Across the street from the car stores were located a bar and restaurant which Dan took me into on several occasions. Next to the bar was a TV and radio store called Wendell's TV. Dan worked for Wendell, the owner. I remember Wendell as a young white man, about 30 years old and friendly to me with a ready smile. He had sandy blonde hair and was a little taller than Dan. He was husky and muscular. I remember Dan taking me into the TV store and seeing all the new television sets. I guess they were called sets in the early 1950's because, if you could afford to buy one of these incredible technological devices, you set it on top of a table to watch. Television was a brand new technology in the early 1950's whose origins can be traced back to Nicholas Tesla. I remember that Dan and Helen had discussed the dangers of working for the TV store. His job involved climbing onto roofs in the area and installing small portable aluminum and plastic television antennas to receive TV signals from NBC and CBS broadcasting towers, located atop Cheyenne Mountain near Colorado Springs. Dan brought home, on several occasions, some of the brown plastic cable wires and the 4-inch-long TV roof screws, that held the cable running from the rooftop antenna and down the roof and into the customer's home. I remember playing with these aluminum and brown plastic screws because they looked like a 4-inch lollipop.

Walking west on the sidewalk, from the TV store, a person would come to the center of town which was a paved road. At this point, when I was a child, if you looked right or North, I saw for a distance of a couple of blocks. These two blocks contained small one or two story mom and pop stores. When I looked left or south down the main street, I would see some larger two story buildings for two or three blocks. There was a small park with grass on the west side of the street and it had either an army mobile canon or a white and green army missile on display in the park. On the same side of the street, next to the park, stood a two story building that housed a Rexall Pharmacy and the classic soda fountain with a soda jerk dressed in a white uniform. Next to the pharmacy, was the Chief Theater with its traditional Indian chief with headdress sign and all the yellow lights to attract moviegoers. These 6 main businesses, in the center of Rocky Ford, and the park were the major locations that I knew about when I was 4 years old and older. There were two other grocery stores and one building that scared me. When Dan and Helen moved me and Patricia to Rocky Ford a lot of events would transpire that, decades later, I would begin to understand when I began to do my Bigfoot, UFO research.

When we moved to Rocky Ford I can only remember playing and interacting with two other kids: Patricia and my uncle David, who was about 8 years older than me. David was the youngest son of George and Jocobh, Dan's parents and my grandparents. Dan's siblings were, in order of age: Joseph, Barbara, Ray, George, Jess, Dan, Ledia and David. Helen's siblings, in order of age: Paul, Ernie, Mary, Helen and Bennie. When Dan and Helen moved me and Patricia to Rocky Ford, as I said earlier, I have no memory of Don, Glenn or Tim. In a normal family of five children and two parents there would be lots of talking, yelling, playing, cuts and bruises, and playing with next door neighbor kids. A household full of small children would be a very busy and noisy place; a place in time, in which I, as the oldest kid, would remember the physical and vocal interactions of five kids and two parents. As I mentioned earlier, we moved to Rocky Ford, into a mysterious home near George and Jocobh. I am in no way certain of this and is only a guess. This home was small and I remember it being a one story tall dark brown stucco home. There were five or six concrete steps on the front door with a small roof covered porch the length of the front of the home. This home was tall because the five or six steps means this home was 36 inches above the ground. There were large mature trees at the backyard and all around the home there was thick, lush, green, wild grass and scattered bushes. It is odd because I don't remember any other homes nearby. I barely remember a road in front of the house.

I can remember one time being outside during the day, the sky was dark and I vividly remember the air was hot, thick and muggy. I had a small little model WWII airplane and I was playing like I was flying the airplane. I may have been four years old. Even at that age, I thought to myself that something strange was happening where I was at. I remember that I was having trouble breathing. Something happened that day such as a nearby tornado or a strong storm.

At that home, a family showed up that I met. It was a Rocky Ford family of four. The father was Charlie, the mother was Dottie, the daughter was named Dodo, and their son was called Chucky. On several occasions, the family visited with us at our strange wetlands house. The parents were very happy, friendly people. Dodo and Chuckie were my age of four and five. They both had brown freckles in a line below their eyes, as did their mother. I liked playing with Chucky and Dodo. After I had seen them for 3 or 4 times, I never saw them again.

I called the house strange where I met the Milier family because the property seemed to be perpetually wet with underground water. It was as though the home had been built on a wetlands area. One summer morning, around 1954, I was on the right side of the home and there was a water hydrant sticking up out of the ground, about 10 feet from the house. The hydrant was about 3 feet tall. I turned the round wheel and out came water and a small 12 inch snake. Inside this home, at the back of the house, on the floor, was a black steel grate that looked down into what must have been the gas heater. I remember getting on my stomach and looking down into the grate and getting really scared when I saw black water around some kind of machine down there. This device could also have been a sump pump.

It was at this house that I first met Helen's father, John. Her father showed up at our home one evening and I was very impressed with this 45-year-old man. He came into the house when Helen opened the front door. He was very loud and boisterous and came into the house with a sort of sleeping bag or thick camping blanket, as well as, a beautiful amber and brown guitar. He was dressed in a manner that filled me with awe.

He had on a red rugged looking cowboy shirt with new Levi's pants and a cowboy belt. Topping off his outfit, he wore a white cowboy hat. I had never seen or heard a person like John. Helen introduced her dad to me and he grabbed my hand and said, "Hi Danny! Nice to meet you!" He had a distinct inflection in his voice, almost like a mild foreign accent. In later years, as a teenager, I saw John two other times but I never asked Helen about her dad's voice. That evening, when John showed up at our home, the lamp lights were on shining on the light brown terracotta inside living room walls. That evening, there was a beautiful amber glow where John sat down on the wood floor. I had never encountered anyone like him. He sat down on the wood floor and motioned for me to come over to him. He proceeded to open up and spread out his big brown heavy blanket. He carefully pulled out a Winchester 30-30 that looked brand new. I looked at it with amazement. He said, 'Here! Hold it" as he put his hands under the rifle, in case I dropped it. I held the heavy rifle for a moment. I felt myself beaming as he took back his Winchester. He set the 30-30 down on the blanket and said, "What do we have here? Lookey! Lookey!" I looked at his hands as he put them into the blanket. He gently pulled out another rifle which looked much different and thinner. "Lookey, Danny! This is yours to shoot!" John had given me his Winchester .22 caliber single shot rifle. Helen protested that a four year old should not have a gun or something to that effect. John insisted and that settled the matter. I was happy and excited as I held the much lighter rifle. Things were about to get even more exciting. "Lookey! Lookey!" John said to me as he pulled a large bank bag from the blanket. Suddenly, this amazing grizzled cowboy man was emptying what looked like thousands of every denomination of coins, as well as bills. At four, I knew that adults used coins and paper dollars to buy groceries and candy at the store. The sight of all this money, to a little kid like me, was amazing. I am sure that my little mouth and eyes were open wide as I got down on the blanket, on hands and knees, and stared at the treasure trove of coins and cash. John said, "Here Danny! Go ahead and look and see what you want! Don't be shy." He laughed a lot and so did Helen as they watched me lift up the coins and cash in my little hands and let it fall back onto the blanket. When I think back on that night, long ago, in the amber glow of the mysterious house; an impressionable little boy with wonder in his eyes and mind, learned a life lesson that would follow me all my life. I picked out a couple of dollars and coins and was very happy. The ancients believe that when we are born we are given our fates. On that night, a family member who was a stranger to me, shared gifts with me and it is a lesson that I have never forgotten. The noble human idea that you treat your family with love, respect, dignity, empathy and understanding.

After awhile, John pulled out his beautiful guitar and sang a song. I was mesmerized by the musical talents of this old cowboy. At this time, I did not know what Grandpa John did for a living. When I got older, Helen would tell me much more about him and his wanderlust. My Grandfather, John, was a sheepherder in Colorado.

When I was living at the mystery home with Dan and Helen I cannot remember ever seeing Pat, who would have been two and a half to three years old, yet I can remember Charlie, Dottie, Dodo and Chucky visiting a number of times. The fact is, I can hardly remember seeing Helen or Dan at this home. It is as though I lived alone. I don't believe we lived there very long maybe 2 months.

Chapter 2 ROCKY FORD

The next events that I can recall is living or visiting with Dan's parents, George and Jocobh, who lived one block south of Highway 50 next to the train tracks, about 1 mile from downtown Rocky Ford. 1/2 block east of their small white stucco home, around a 90 degree curve in the road that turned south, was a very scary water building. This building must have been about 50 feet long. It was about two stories tall and was made of dark brown wood planks. It looks like there were three giant hot tubs on the top of the flat roof. The entire building facing our home had a wood louvre construction, in which water would fall from the top of the roof down the side of the building, and into some sort of pool at the bottom of the building. This foreboding building, with its water sounds, scared me. It was at this little home of Jocobh and George that I can remember a lot more interaction with adults and other kids. At the cream colored home, next to Highway 50, I can barely remember Helen and Dan except in the little grocery store across the street. This little home was shaped like an L. The house set on a medium sized lot with big mature shade trees with no grass, except prairie grass here and there. There were no trees on the property except on the north end where the dirt road, running east and west, parallel with the train tracks, turned into a dirt driveway at the backyard. Pat and I were at this home for a lot of time. I can remember being at the back door next to the driveway and walking along what led into a well lit light blue living room. Turning left for a shorter distance were 2 bedrooms. The back door led to a long thin kitchen that had a small black pot belly wood stove. I remember there being a large metal can with fresh cut long yellow firewood with a pungent smell. This kitchen area was rather dark compared to the light blue living room. They had a well, in which a person would hand pump the big hand pump in the kitchen floor. Jocobh always had a 2 gallon silvery galvanized bucket with clear cold delicious water.

In the summer time, the sweltering hot temperatures made Pat and I drink with a ladle from that bucket, all the time. A number of remarkable events happened to me when Pat and I were living at this home. Many times Pat and I would be in the front yard playing on the ground next to the dirt road that ran north and south. As the road headed south for two blocks, it intercepted a water canal that was about six or eight feet wide with a walking foot bridge spanning the canal. There were handrails, supports and metal mesh to keep a person from falling in. I recall, that on many hot summer days, Pat, who was 3 years old, and I would be outside unsupervised all day long, going in and out of the house, just like at the other houses. Pat and I wandered the neighborhood unsupervised by adults. I can remember Helen, a couple times at best, in the kitchen where Grandma Jocobh baked on a big black wood fired stove. I cannot remember seeing Dan but maybe once. I remember that Jocobh and George's youngest son was David, my dad's youngest brother and my uncle, who was about eight or nine years old. Jocobh must have been an old woman in those days to have such a young son. She looked like a tiny version of Albert Einstein as she always sat in her living room chair. She would sit there on her favorite chair dressed in her little flowered print cotton dress with an apron on. She would be smoking unfiltered Camel cigarettes and she had the sad little Einstein expression on her face all the time. When I ran into the living room, she called to me in and then the sad expression would turn into a smile as I sat on her lap. Smoking the Camel cigarettes had made her teeth a light brown and both she and George always had a faint odor of sweat, as there was no air conditioning. I recall being outside with her on the side of the house and she was showing me the hollyhocks, azaleas and sunflowers. She reached down and picked dark green mint flowers for her tea. Another thing that she did a lot in the chair was to cover one nostril with her finger and take deep sniffs of rubbing alcohol with the other nostril. I never saw grandpa George or Jocobh drink alcohol. I could tell that this grandma really loved Pat and I by the way she smiled at us. At this home, I have no memory at all of Don, Glen or Timothy. Patricia and David were the only kids I saw.

In the living room were some high shelves that I could not reach. They contained three or four model airplanes that belonged to David. I always wanted to play with these models. One day Jocobh took down the F-86 Saber Jet model. I was playing with it and suddenly David walked into the room and saw me with his model. He immediately began shouting and screaming at me and then began to cry. I gave the model to him and he did not hit me.

Even as a child I noticed that all over the Masias' property and the neighborhood there were beautiful wild sunflowers and Jocobh grew large commercial sunflowers with the edible sunflower seeds. These wild growing flowers had a wonderful pungent odor. Bees were everywhere pollinating and feeding on these flowers. Many days Pat and I would be outside picking the petals of the flowers. On a number of occasions Patricia would sit on the ground picking the petals of sunflowers. Something in my little mind told me that these beautiful sunflowers were very important to me. Decades later, the fact that Jocobh looked like a little Einstein and Einstein solved the $E=MC2$ equation, when he discovered that mercury orbits the Sun and its orbit leaves a geometric pattern that looks like a sunflower around the Sun. These two facts combined in the 1980's to tie into my Bigfoot, alien research, which is ultimately connected to the stars in the universe and Einstein's theory of relativity.

Back in the 1950's, candy cost one penny and was called penny candy. Somehow I found, or someone in the house gave me, pennies because I did not have grandpa John's coins. There were two grocery stores within 2 to 4 blocks of the house. One grocery store was 2 blocks south across the 8 foot irrigation canal and a little bit further south. I remember it was a one story white building with a 1 X 8 wood siding. I used to go there many times, by myself, with pennies to buy candy. It is amazing that I was not kidnapped, run over by a car, attacked by a dog or slipped into the deep canal and drowned. The other grocery store was located in the opposite direction across the dirt road, then a dry field infested with mounds of red fire ants, and across active dangerous train tracks. This was a gas station grocery store. This was the time when the Russians launched Sputnik into orbit. The little Sputnik chewing gum balls were about the size of a quarter and were a light blue, covered in small granular sugar crystals.

I remember going to this store and a train was coming at me from east to west. I am four years old standing about 8 feet from a moving train going about 10 to 20 miles per hour. The ground is rumbling under my tiny feet as I crane my head to look up at the top of the train. It was a very frightening experience the first time. Several other times, I had the train experience and I saw open side doors with hobo men yelling and laughing at me. It's amazing that the train did not run over me.

Right next door to the Masias home was a small light powder blue stucco home. The same color as the living room. I used to always stare at it and wonder why there were white crescent moons, stars and sunbursts painted all over the small house. I never saw anybody there so Patricia and I played in the front yard all the time. These painted symbols, like Indian pictographs of the universe, were about 18 inches in diameter. As I said earlier, my Bigfoot, UFO research has led me to the Sun and the stars in the universe. In 1954, at Jocobh's home, a whole series of amazing synchronistic events all came together that would follow me all my life, protecting me and would ultimately be my legacy. Jocobh looked like a tiny version of the elderly Einstein. Everywhere outside were the sunflowers that Einstein said Mercury made as it orbits the Sun. Grandma smoked Camel cigarettes. The camel logo denotes the pyramids. In the Egyptian religion, Heliopolis was the center of worship for the supreme Sun God Ra. The light blue home next door was painted by fate by someone recognizing the universe which Einstein is connected to.

Another astonishing synchronistic event happened to me in the summer of 1954. Earlier I said that I would just wander off for 3 or 4 or 8 blocks and Dan, Helen or grandma knew nothing about it. Grandpa George, earlier that spring had taken me on several walks. In the summer, he took me on a walking excursion, holding my hand, to downtown Rocky Ford. He took me to the movie house and I saw Walt Disney's Brer Rabbit. After that, he took me to the pharmacy soda fountain and introduced me to his friend. Later that day, we stayed for a parade down Main Street.

Driving with my dad in the car and walking with Grandpa, I learned the route to take to go downtown. I remember driving in an old black car that looked like a big Volkswagen. One summer day, I started wandering away from the house. I ended up downtown across the street from the theater on Main Street. As I was walking on the sidewalk, suddenly an all grayish white figure appeared in front of me like a ghost. This humanoid figure was a little taller than me with large black oval eyes, with a large head and skinny body. This little creature scared me really bad. We both stood there for three minutes or so and we stared at each other. After minutes of visual eye to eye contact, the little creature boy calmed me down and made me go back home. Years later, as an adult, I know that this was an alien that did not want me to walk any further because of some unknown danger to me. I returned home safely after my encounter with the alien.

During the time that Patricia and I were in Rocky Ford it was Grandma Jocobh who I remember taking care of us. I remember Helen a few times but little Einstein Jocobh made a big impression on me. Over the years, as I have thought about that time in my young life, Dan, Helen, Don, Glen and Tim must have been living somewhere else. They would periodically come to Grandma's house and pick me up in their old car and we would go somewhere. Dan and Helen were not wealthy parents. Over the years they told me that he was a contractor who drove a 2 ton truck and hauled watermelons, cantaloupes, potatoes, onions, etc., for farmers under contract. Helen and Dan both told me that they worked as laborers in the blazing hot farm fields of Rocky Ford, picking cantaloupes, onions, watermelons etc. They said it was brutally hard backbreaking labor that paid very low wages. If they worked from sunup to sundown they could explain why I did not see them. Years later, Dan told me that he and his brothers Joseph, Ray, George and their dad George were business partners in a bar restaurant called The Picquick Inn. I have a faint memory of going there in downtown Rocky Ford. As I walked in the front door, on the left, was a row of five light yellow booths going straight back to the end of the building. On the right side, was a bar counter top with about 8 or 10 stools fixed to the floor. Dan told me that on one occasion a young male had entered the bar and was shooting with a .38 caliber handgun at him. This mysterious man was trying to kill Dan. He said he was running and ducking from the bullets. I had asked Dan why this man tried to kill him. He was evasive and wouldn't answer my question.

It was at the same time that Dan and his brother, Joseph, and a black man named Tyler went into the dancehall business in Rocky Ford. I believe that the name of the dance hall was called the Otero Dance Hall. It was located northeast of downtown in a rural area. I recall standing in the old car as Dan, Helen, Patricia and me slowly drove up to a whitish dirt parking lot of the dancehall. It was a light brown color, one story structure with a typical roof of the time. The hall was about 50 feet wide and 100 feet long. There were several steps up to the front double doors. As we walked through the front doors one afternoon, the building seemed huge to me. It had beautiful hardwood oak flooring. I remember the floor looked light cream colored. I looked up to the ceiling of this beautiful building, which came to an apex like the top of a pyramid. The stage where the bands played was at the far end of the building and was about 2 feet tall. Just as a person entered the building to the left was a white storage room filled with brown cardboard boxes of Coors and Walters beer bottles. There were some broken beer bottles and the spilled beer gave off a strong odor. I had never been in such a large building with room to run everywhere. It was very exciting. Ten years or so later, Dan told me at the Mission Bell that he and his brothers and a black man named Tyler operated a Dance Hall in Rocky Ford. Apparently, has black partner Tyler had connections in the big band world of the 1940's and 50's. They were able to book some big bands of that day including Duke Ellington's band of nationwide fame. For years, an 11 X 8 inch, black and white photo of Dan, posing with Duke Ellington and his band hung over the fireplace at the Mission Bell. As well as, a signed football from Bart Starr, the Green Bay quarterback.

Years later, as a grown man, I thought about what I saw and experienced. Dan and Helen went from back breaking harvesting by hand in the nearby fields to becoming a contractor business man driving a big truck. They then must have had a lot of money because they started The Picquick Bar and Grill and then started a dance hall business. None of these businesses was cheap to get into even in those days. Dan told me, as a teenager that he was in business with his brothers. Years later Helen let it slip to me that these two businesses had saddled her and Dan with big unpaid bills to Coors and the Walter Brewing Company. Neither Dan or Helen ever wanted to talk about these two business adventures when I asked them questions as a young teenager. When I inquired about their glory days in Rocky Ford I sensed that they were hiding something from the past from these businesses and other things. For instance, every time my uncle George and his wife Sally visited us at the Mission Bell, Dan, Helen, George and Sally would only speak Spanish. They did not want me to know what they were talking about. At the time, I did not know it, but Dan and Helen were, or became, secretive and deceptive and this would have a big effect on me later in my life.

It was at this time of the dancehall visit and Picquick Bar visits that I had that I encountered another unexplained event. One sunny late summer day I was standing in the driveway at the side backyard. For some reason I looked up and above me, about 15 feet in the air, was a thin crescent shaped object. The ends of the crescent were pointed at the ground. There was some kind of geometric writing on the object which was about 2 or 3 feet wide. This hovering object had a patina that was dull gold and a light burnished brown. It was a beautiful object. By the time that I saw this beautiful object, I had numerous encounters with the unknown. It was Karma and fate that I was born in a region known for it's amazing crops. Without the Sun and photosynthesis, mankind and animals could not exist. Years later, my scientific research would lead right to the Sun.

Chapter 3 **PUEBLO**

It was at this time that Dan and Helen moved me, Pat, Donald, Glen and Tim to Pueblo, Colorado in the late summer or early fall of 1955. This is the first time that I can remember seeing all the younger boys in the same house with me and Pat. They moved us into a tiny home with a large picture window on the left of the front door. This home was located on Uintah Street on the far eastern boundary of the city. The house was about two or three blocks south of a school called Spann Elementary. This is the first school I ever attended as a kindergartner. I clearly remember that the weather was hot and then, on two occasions, a broadcasting musical ice cream truck came on the road and stopped in front of our home. The exciting musical beat brought the neighborhood kids running to the white truck with light colored yellow windows. The young guy driving the ice cream truck wore a white uniform with a white cap. He sold flavored ice snow cones, ice cream, popcorn and candy. Most of the Masias kids were eagerly outside the delightful truck. None of us had any coins or money. A few other older neighbor kids and teenagers bought snow cones and ice cream. I was 5 years old and looking at the Masias kids and me dressed in poor children's clothes. This is the first time in my very young life and with all these other Masias kids, that I realized I was very poor. Another time, a photo peddler came to our door and the neighborhood with a little brown horse. I think that Helen put me on the horse and the guy photographed me. Over the years I was not able to get this photo of me.

At the Uintah home in Pueblo I continued my wandering wander-lust, just like in Rocky Ford without any adult supervision. Three blocks south of our home, on the same side of the road, was a drive in movie theater called the Arcadia Drive In located next to a Highway 50. Across Highway 50 from the drive in was a long one story yellow grocery store. I remember crossing the busy Highway 50 without being killed by a car and going to the grocery store. I loved it inside the store. There was much more merchandise inside than the Rocky Ford stores. I remember picking up little metal model Ford cars as big as my hand from 1955. These models looked like the real cars driving on the roads. Across the street, at the drive in, I recall standing next to the 6-foot red fence and poking my head through a broken section and watching a color movie and seeing all the parked cars in the drive in.

At this time, it had to have been 8:30 or 8:45 p.m. in the summer when it starts getting dark. I was 5 years old wandering around at that time with no adult supervision. It is remarkable that I was not killed. One evening I was outside in front of our home next to the road. Suddenly, I heard the most bloodcurdling animal sound I ever heard (except for the Bigfoot scream I heard in 2001). I turned and saw a medium sized black dog on fire running up the road right next to me and headed towards the school. It was a positively horrible scream and horrendous sight to see an innocent dog running down the road on fire. When I look back on this event, it was an ominous omen of events to come. Living in Pueblo, Colorado from 1955 to 1965 would profoundly affect me for the rest of my life. Pueblo was called the Steel City and astrophysicists have discovered that all the heavy elements of the earth, including iron which steel is made up of, came from a giant exploding star or supernova billions of years ago. For me, growing up in Pueblo would be a dangerous gritty, bloody and mystifying experience with all the barrios, pachucos, desperately poor people, gang violence and mean adults.

It was at the Uintah house that Dan, Helen, Pat, Don, Glenn, Tim and I lived in a tiny brown house. Helen was pregnant with Sam and gave birth to him in Pueblo. All of us kids slept on couches or rollaway beds in the front living room. I remember laying on a bed with kids sleeping all around me. There was a large picture window and as cars outside drove past the home their headlights would cast long light ghostly shadows from one end of the living room to the other end. It really scared me every night as I watched the ghostly light shadows dance back and forth. Years later, as I conducted my research, these light shadows would return to me in the form of infrared night vision photos, showing light energy alien creatures. The ghostly beams of nocturnal lights, I would later realize, decades later, as showing the way for Albert Einstein to discover the theory of relativity.

In the fall of 1955 I first attended grade school, two blocks north of our home, called Spann public school. I vividly remember being afraid to go to school and Helen walked me to school the first day of kindergarten. It was a beautiful morning as Helen and I walked up to the side of the beautiful red brick and concrete structure. I remember lots of exciting happy little kids milling all about and it was very intimidating because I had never seen so many nicely dressed white kids with blonde, brown and red hair. I remember a small group of boys had little toy cars and they were throwing them up an angled concrete floor against the outside school wall. Gravity would make the little cars roll back down to them. I was very frightened that day at school, at first, but then I calmed down and things were okay. I remember that Helen took me into this breathtaking beautiful one story building. She took me to the kindergarten class and I sat down at a school desk. My teacher was the most beautiful young woman I had ever seen. She was a tall blonde young woman and on that first day she wore a dark forest green dress. After my initial fear of school, I quickly learned to love going to school and learning. Everyday, I could not wait to go to school in the morning. I've never experienced anything like it. Nobody read school books to me or tried to teach me the alphabet or how to write my name, so when I entered school my little spirits soared. I loved my teacher more than my parents so when they pulled me out of Spann school and my teachers class I was unhappy with my parents. At the time, I was a student with my first teacher and I did not know that there would be a mystery surrounding my teacher. Years later, in Pueblo, at Goodnight public school, a young blonde girl who looked just like my first grade teacher would reappear to say hello to me and look at me with a long faraway look. This mysterious young beautiful girl would follow me for the rest of my life to Woodland Park, Colorado, near Hondo where I spotted the Bigfoots and started doing my research into aliens. For now she will remain a mystery.

I attended Spann school for several months and was very mad at Dan and Helen when we began to move out of the Uintah home. We moved to a place called The Projects in western Pueblo, next to a Catholic orphanage and cemetery. Sometime in November or December 1955, Dan and Helen moved the entire Masias family into a large public assistance location of many two story, red brick apartment buildings. I never knew the details of the large concentrations of buildings but my understanding is that it was for poor people. To me this place was like heaven after living at the Uintah home that had all dirt streets and no grass in the yards. The Spann school was a beautiful brick building with grass out front and was by far the best part of the neighborhood.

Moving into The Projects was very beautiful. I recall that the inside of the two story apartment had white walls and a beautiful kitchen with new wood cabinets. There was a steep stairway to two upstairs bedrooms and we had a very nice new bathroom. Outside, there was thick green sod grass and concrete side walks and all the streets everywhere were paved. I thought this was a great place to live. The Projects were maybe five years old and were located near a shopping center called the Sunset Plaza. There was a Safeway grocery store and a store I loved called Western Auto. It was an auto parts store that sold many beautiful bikes. On the other side of The Projects was a U.S. Navy gray colored building with a small P.T. boat in the front yard. The small complex was surrounded by an 8 foot tall chain link fence. I always wondered why this navy place was there and not near the ocean. On the west side of The Projects were two large empty dirt properties with wild native plants and a scattering of fireant hills. Across the street, or south of our brick apartment, was a large beautiful brick building that was a Catholic orphanage. On a number of occasions, my parents had sent me over to this building for catechism classes. I remember my Catholic catechism study book that I was given by the people at the orphanage. My folks had told me that this beautiful building was an orphanage for poor children who had somehow been abandoned or had lost their parents. I remember feeling pathos and feeling sorry for the kids over there. But there was a mystery concerning the orphanage. In all the times I went there for catechism classes I never saw or heard any sign of orphaned children. The only kids I saw were my fellow catechism class mates. On the orphanage property, due east, was a small football field. In three or four years in the future I would return to the football field and play a football game for Sacred Heart Catholic School. Next to the football field was a cemetery. As a passenger in my parents old automobile I saw the cemetery many times.

I remember that the Masias family spent the 1955 Christmas at the public projects in Pueblo, Colorado. I can still remember that Christmas in my mind. It was at this time that something very mysterious in my mind happened to me. It happened in the spring of 1956 when I was attending Minnequa grade school. I was 7 years old and I was walking one quarter mile to Minnequa grade school. One morning in April of 1956, as I headed off to school, I was crossing one of the fields on my way to school. Suddenly, I saw a blinding white light and felt an excruciating blow to the back of my head. I feel like someone had hit the back of my head with a hammer. To this day, I have a small lump on the back of my head where a mysterious object struck the back of my head. Over the years I have thought about this event and wondered about what struck the back of my head in 1956. I have come to the conclusion that I may have been struck by a tiny meteorite falling from the sky that spring morning in 1956. I was screaming and in pain and touching the back of my head as I ran home to the projects. My right hand was covered in blood. On this spring day in Pueblo, I could have died but again some great benevolent power was protecting me.

The Masias family was at The Projects of Pueblo for two years or so, from the summer of 1956 to the summer of 1958. While at The Projects, I had six siblings: Patricia, Donald, Glenn, Timothy, Sam and Benjamin by the fall of 1957. In the summer of 1958, Dan and Helen moved the Masias family from the Pueblo projects, near the Sunset Shopping Center, up north and further west to a location just outside Pueblo city limits, near an open water storage facility. This was a small home on a street next to train tracks where hobos used to come to our back door asking for a meal or to do yard work to earn money. From the back of this tiny home, about 300 feet away, were three large square concrete open water storage facilities. On a number of occasions I went down there past the train tracks. The water was very scary looking and I never went back there. This area of Pueblo County also had a small wetlands area next to the road about 2 blocks away from my home. It was a small pond about 50 feet in diameter and it had green pond scum on its surface. It was a scary site and I never played there. This area of Pueblo, when the Masias family lived there, was hot, dry and desert like, so the small pond never made sense to me. The entire community and its residents at that time we're extremely poor and living in third world conditions. Streets were not paved and there was sporadic water and sewer service.

An elderly white man, named Velers, rented this tiny home to the Masias family. Next door to this home my uncle George, older brother to my dad, Dan, then had an auto service repair garage business. Next to my uncles garage business was a small grocery store where my folks shopped sometimes. Across the street and west of our house, my uncle George's mother in law lived named Mrs. Aragon. Her two sons, Jake and Elmer, and her blonde daughter, Rose, lived there with her. I always remember Elmer because he was a nice young teenage guy who was nice to me. It was at this time that I was 9 years old and Elmer must have been 15 or 16 years old. He helped me with my bicycle repairs and showed me his model cars. For two years, from 1959 to 1960, I attended Sacred Heart Catholic school in Pueblo. A yellow school bus picked me up near our home early every morning. I attended Mass every day before going to school classes.

We lived at the Velers Home for one year and then Dan and Helen moved us five blocks west from this home to another home from 1959 to 1960. I still attended Sacred Heart Catholic school and Patricia and Donald attended Hyde Park grade school which was one mile away. Dan and Helen could not afford to send me, Patricia and Donald to Catholic school so they settled on me, the oldest son. Young Father Sierra, who was our parish priest at the local church, made some sort of financial arrangements with the Sacred Heart Catholic school authorities and my parents which allowed me to attend the Catholic school system. It was at this time, in 1960, that Father Sierra received an archaeology artifact from people in Grand Junction, Colorado. The artifact was related to King Constantine, Helena and the Conquisitors. It would influence my research and scientific discovery fifty some years later when the Denver Post and Independent N.P. would discover the artifact.

In retrospect, as I think back over the years, it was fate that has ruled my life. From the earliest time, when I was one year old, I was in constant contact with some kind of water source. From the water cooling towers, Lake Holbrook and canals of Rocky Ford to Pueblo's water storage reservoirs and the falls in Green Mountain Falls, Colorado. Water has been a constant companion in my life. It is the physical properties of water which is composed of H_2O: hydrogen and oxygen. Hydrogen being the most abundant light gas in the universe and the gaseous substance that the stars are made up of. This, in turn, leads to my scientific discovery about our own Sun or star and what exists there and by inference the rest of the universe. In my life, fate has been the overwhelming force that has ruled my life and the purpose of this book.

In the summer of 1960, Dan and Helen moved our family down south and west off Thatcher Street to a small home on Cactus Street.

During the time when our family moved from Rocky Ford, Colorado to Pueblo my father had worked in the public service industry. He worked at a Mexican restaurant called Valencia's, owned by Tom. My dad managed this restaurant for a number of years and then Tom bought a second restaurant called Sebastians. He then managed this restaurant for a number of years. Valencia's was located on a road that led to the Steel Mill. Sebastian's was located near the Minnequa Lake in Pueblo.

In the summer of 1960, when we moved to the tiny house on Cactus Street, my dad, Dan, went to work for the Walter Brewing Company of Pueblo and an old white man named Kerling. The Masias family lived at the Cactus address for 2 years from 1960 to 1962. I was going into the fifth grade at Goodnight Elementary School near our Cactus home. It was at this school that I would experience 6 profound events that would follow me through life. I would not realize the importance of these experiences until I built my home in Green Mountain Falls in the 1980s.

By 1960 my mother, Helen, had given birth to baby Mark. This part of Pueblo County was a poor area but not as bad as the Dog patch area that we had just left. There are three streets that I vividly remember Pear, Cactus, and Cherry Lane. I was 11 years old and going into the 5th grade and Cherry Lane homes and properties really made me realize how poor my family was. Pear, Cactus and Cherry Lane streets were west of Thatcher Road. In 1960, this area of Pueblo County was a small area (of about a mile by a mile) of poor white people. Some homes were underground homes. A mile south and east of this area wealthy people or middle class people of the 1960's lived. It was at that time, when I was 11 years old and going to the 5th grade at Goodnight Elementary school, that my life would change. In the fall of 1960, when I began attending Goodnight Elementary school, one third of the 200 students attending the school where children of poor families. A small enclave of depressed housing with poor white families surrounded Goodnight grade school. The "rich" kids, and by this I mean lower to middle class, lived east of Thatcher Avenue, near the city swimming pool and City Golf Course. I am certain that the Masias family were the poorest children attending Goodnight school in fall 1960.

My parents took me to Pueblo thrift stores where they bought secondhand school clothes. We also bought books there for five cents or a quarter. At an early age, I learned to love books and reading and both my parents told me stories about the ancient Egyptians, Greeks, Etruscans and Romans. I enjoyed the stories about Plato, Aristotle, Socrates and Marcus Aurelius. I learned from a very early age that I loved the ancient world and I liked to read about man's history. From 1960 to 1962, I attended the fifth and sixth grade at Goodnight Elementary, a school named after the famous 18th century Texas cattle baron, Charles Goodnight, and who inspired the Lonesome Dove TV series.

The first of the significant events that happened to me was reading a book. It was at Goodnight school that my teacher, Miss Stefanik, a good caring teacher, recognized my interest in books. Miss Stefanik, the school librarian, helped me to check out books. One of the first books I read was titled The Boy Who Found the Light, by Dale Dearmond. Keep in mind, this is 1960 and it is only 15 years since the beginning of the Atomic Age, when the United States dropped an atomic bomb on Hiroshima. By 1955, Robert Oppenheimer and Albert Einstein, both associated with the atomic bomb, are against the existence of atomic weapons, but do recognize that atomic power can be used to generate electricity for society. I am sure the author of this children's book wrote it with atomic energy in the back of his mind. I cannot be 100% certain of the exact contents of this children's book, but I can say that, one day, a young boy was outside his home playing and he caught a glimpse of a white light. Later, after time had passed, he discovered the beautiful blue light at his home and it turned out to be an important source of energy for people. At the time, when I was in the 5th grade and 11 years old,

I was amazed by this children's X-files book for 1960. When I read the book, The Boy Who Found the Light, I was enthralled with it. Deep in my young mind, it touched and opened a door that I could not understand until I built my home in the 1980's, when my scientific research would discover a blue light. The theme of this book was all the more fascinating to me because my folks had told me that the army had recovered a crashed UFO at Roswell, New Mexico. They also told me about the scientific genius Albert Einstein and what he had discovered about space, stars and the universe. Four years earlier, a young guy at The Projects, named Mickey, had told me wondrous stories about the universe. Thereafter, my love and thirst for knowledge about the universe never left me.

The second event that happened to me at Goodnight school was when I was in Miss Bell's social studies class, I read a book on Greek mythology which fell in line with what my parents had taught me about the ancient Greeks. In the fall of 1960, I read a book that showed the Greek Atlas, a muscular giant as big as the earth, holding up the Earth from below our planet. I read the story of Atlas and read it again because the story was just so fantastic. How in Greek mythology could a giant man creature bigger than the earth exist? The image and story of Atlas was so fantastic to me that it stuck with me all of my life. Later in my life, when I built my home and was engaged in my Bigfoot and alien research, after 2001, my astonishing scientific discovery revealed that humanoid creatures the size of Atlas do exist!

The third big event that I experienced, but at the time did not know the importance and validity of it, was the winter of 1961 at Goodnight grade school. The school held an annual science fair and I decided to do a science project on the scientific importance of Earth's volcanoes. I made a volcano out of paraffin wax about 12 inches in circumference and 8 inches tall. It sat on a cardboard platform with a little village and trees, bushes, lakes, creeks, roads and the elements of civilization. My science project on volcanoes quoted Pompeii and

Vesuvius eruptions and that volcanoes can affect civilizations and mankind. The science teacher and judges gave ribbons of science achievement to other students. My volcano science project was ignored and did not win any science awards. Since 1961 geologists have discovered a super volcano at Yellowstone in Wyoming, a scant 600 miles north of Pueblo, Colorado. In 2003, I self published my scientific research on volcanoes around the earth and their influence on human affairs. It was titled Passage to Ascension - Where the Next Disasters and Terrorism Will Strike in the US, by Daniel Masiasmuh sigh uh. My scientific work in this book has turned out to be very accurate in its predictions about events all over the globe.

The fourth extremely important event that I experienced at Goodnight school was in the winter of 1962. Again, it was the science fair, and this time my science project would be about the Golden Gate suspension bridge in California. The idea was that without the Roman arch and bridges of the ancient and modern world and the science that went into them; the modern world wouldn't exist. My father took me to a lumber yard near Minnequa Lake in Pueblo. He bought the small lumber and wire parts for a 3-foot long replica of the Golden Gate suspension bridge. I drew up plans from a photo of the bridge and my dad advised me on how to construct the model bridge. When the Science Fair was held, again my science project was ignored. However, like the science fair before, with my volcano, a lot of Goodnight students told me my volcano and bridge science projects were really cool. As fate would have it, again I would not know how important my Golden Gate Bridge science project was until the 1980's when I built my home in Green Mountain Falls Colorado and began to do my Bigfoot - alien research.

In 2014, I published some of my groundbreaking scientific information in the local Gazette newspaper. The scientific article spoke of some of the astonishing infrared night vision photos of aliens in a Stargate bridge that I have discovered on our archaeological home site. Einstein- Rosen bridges or Stargates were also discussed prominently in my scientific newspaper article. Just as in 1962, when I was 12 years old at Good night elementary school and I built a model replica of the Golden Gate Bridge, it was my fate 40 years later, when I built my home, that I would discover an Einstein-Rosen bridge or Stargate on our property.

The fifth fateful event that I experienced at Good night school was in the spring of 1962. I had to go to the principal's office because me and Ray, my friend, had skipped school and went down to the Arkansas River and played all day. For some reason, Larry and a student found out and ratted on us. The next day, I was summoned to principal Smith's office. He gently admonished me for skipping school and proceeded to tell me why it was not right to go along or do what I did the previous day. I was expecting to catch hell from Mr. Smith because he was a young white man who was very muscular and I had heard stories of other kids getting paddled. At that time, Goodnight grade school paddled unruly students to keep discipline at school. I was not looking forward to going to the principal's office because I felt that I may get paddled. That beautiful spring afternoon in May 1962, I slowly walked down the hallway to Mr. Smith's office. As I said, he gently admonished me for skipping school and I was relieved that he did not pull out the dreaded paddle. Mr. Smith was actually pretty nice to me. To this day, I can still remember what Mr. Smith looked like.

Then it happened! I was sitting in a chair listening to Mr. Smith and in walked the most beautiful blonde girl that I have ever seen. My first grade teacher at Spann elementary school was also very pretty but this young girl standing in front of me and looking at me was breathtaking. We both looked at each other. When I turned 11 years old I began to notice girls and when I turned 12 my male hormones began to wake up. I liked a girl in my class named Cathy. I kind of liked her and I think she liked me. I also remember that her big brother threatened to beat me up because I somehow had some "interactions" with his sister Cathy. I never had any kind of contact with Cathy except at school classes at Goodnight. In 1962, Cathy's older brother died of childhood leukemia. A fellow Goodnight student and friend named Bobby, who knew Cathy much better than I did, attended the funeral for Cathy's older brother. Bobby later told me that Cathy was dressed in a black dress and she looked beautiful. In 1960 and 1962 Cathy was a beautiful young, white, brunette girl. She had two best girl friends who were sisters and lived right in front of Goodnight grade school. They were Aileen and Maureen. Every grade school has its kings and queens and Cathy was the queen of Goodnight elementary school in 1961 and 1962. She was a very popular girl and all the boys liked her. She lived 2 blocks away from me at the west end of Pear Street. Once I had seen her older brother, who was taller than her, so when Bobby told me he was going to beat me up, I was scared.

Flashback

I stood there looking at the most beautiful blonde girl had I had ever seen. She was a little bit taller than me. We both stood there for a few moments and stared at each other. I was 12 years old with no experience at all concerning deep emotions of love or heartbreak. But as I stood there looking at her, suddenly instantaneous feelings of a lost love flooded my thoughts. We both emotionally clicked instantly when we saw each other. I experienced an emotional epiphany that took me back in time; something that Albert Einstein might have talked about in space-time conversations. It was as though this young girl and I had been husband and wife and something had happened in the distant ancient past that had separated us. Her and I had a past loving history together and now here we were in May 1962 in the 20th century.

Then principal Smith said, "Daniel this is my daughter, Kristen. Kristen, this is Daniel." We both continued looking at each other and I sensed that Mr. Smith could tell that there was some sort of connection between me and his daughter, Kristen. I stammered a hello to Kristen as we held hands out to shake in greetings. I held her hand for a moment in time. There was a flood of emotions in my young 12 year old mind. To me it was love at first sight! The touch and feel of her hand was magical and glowing. As I held and shook her hand I felt a deep sense of lost love, joy, exhilaration and ecstasy. It was as though a long ago love story had now come full circle, as we looked into each others eyes and held each other's hands in a handshake.

It was then that Mr. Smith said to his daughter, "Daniel is in my office today because he skipped school yesterday. So I have to do something." I looked at Kristen's eyes and her beautiful facial expression and I could tell that she loved me. I knew instantly that if her dad said I had been in a fight and was a bad boy like Elvis Presley she would still be in love with me. After all, I did look like a young Elvis Presley in 1962. Mr. Smith then escorted me to Miss Bell's, my teacher's, class. I was punished by staying after school at 3:15 p.m. and writing 50 times on the class blackboard 'I will never skip school again.' It was May 18, 1962, my birthday, when I met Kristen at Goodnight elementary school. The same birthday as Pope John Paul II, the future Polish Pope in the 1980s, when I built my house in Green Mountain Falls, Colorado.

Goodnight Elementary School in 1962 was a small school of 200 students or less. Many times I had seen principal Smith in the hallway and the gym. He was about six foot tall with a muscular build and he had a short, light blonde marine haircut. I never had any problems with Mr. Smith because I was a well behaved young kid. In fact, I think he liked me and that is why he didn't paddle me for skipping school. He introduced me to his daughter Kristen. He seemed to be happy that he had introduced us to each other and there was a definite connection between us.

During this time we lived at two different homes in the city of Pueblo and two homes in Pueblo County. Being born into a patriarchal family, I, as the oldest son, didn't dare say no or disrespect my father or mother. My father was a young muscular man who worked out. From 1955 to 1964 and beyond, as the oldest son, I was coerced and told by my mother and father that I was going to physically help them take care of, feed and raise their 10 children. I was physically always afraid of my father, until my mid twenties. He had beaten me as a child with a belt. As a teenager he beat me once. As a young teenager I saw him beat up my mother at our home at 3605 West Pikes Peak Avenue, in Colorado Springs. During the years that we lived in Pueblo I was literally forced to become a surrogate father to one sister and seven brothers. I was forced to babysit them, feed them baby bottles, change their dirty diapers, hold them when they were sick or cranky, take them outside and entertain them. I had to help Helen do the large loads of dirty diapers and children's clothes. In those days my family was poor and so my mother and I hung lots of clothes outside most of the year in Pueblo. This laundry work for me never ended. I was also a cook for all these kids. Almost every day I was required to peel, cut and fry potatoes, as well as, prepare the raw flour for making dozens and dozens of tortillas to feed all these children. I also cleaned 25 pound raw pinto beans sacks to cook. I was also forced to clean house on a regular basis, cut weeds, break up concrete with red bricks, water the grass, mow, do yard and home repairs. I never had any help, or very little, from the seven younger kids, even when they became older. My mother and father told me I was the oldest son and that I was going to do this work with a smile on my face.

One winter day heavy snow was falling. After school me, Pat, Don and Glenn walked home after school in heavy snowfall. Don fell behind us, and fell into a deep culvert. We arrived home and realized Don was not with us. I ran back and retraced our steps and found him trapped in the culvert by his foot. I pulled him out and saved him, as my dad came looking for both of us. I believe I saved Don's life that day.

Me, Pat, Don and Glenn all attended Goodnight elementary school. Because our home had no city gas or water service, we had a cistern that ran out of water. Many times, none of us kids could take a bath, and when we did, 8 kids would bathe in the same water, in a small galvanized stock tank; then rinse in clean water. Other kids at school started beating up Pat, Don and Glenn, because of their poor out-of-style clothing and their bad odors. At this time I was in 5th grade. I went and fought with the two kids who were beating up my brothers and sisters and made them stop. Defending these kids gave me a tough boy reputation. A kid named Beau Don, who acted like he was my friend, lied and set me up in a street fist fight with a Pueblo South high school wrestler and football player named Mike. Beau and his brother told him that I was going to beat him up. I was a 5th grader weighing 70 pounds. Mike was in high school and weighed at least 170 pounds. Mike and the two Don brothers came to our house on Cactus Street. Mike confronted me and my mother, Helen, in the back dirt yard. All of my brothers and sister were standing near me and Helen. I told the high school guy I was not going to fight him. Suddenly, Mike slugged me in the face with his fist. My mother, Helen, screamed "Fight him, Danny! Fight him!" Mike continued pounding my head and face with his fists. I fell to the ground in a bloodied, painful and dazed stupor. Mike and the Don brothers walked away laughing at me. My brothers just stood there and looked at me. Helen did not help me up off the ground! People have died from being slugged in the head like this. This happened to me because my parents had told me to protect my brothers and sister from boys at school. When this happened to me this was typical of Pueblo's brutal reputation. I wanted to move from Pueblo. This was the brutal reality of Dogpatch and it almost killed me!

It was also at the Cactus home that my mother, Helen, went through some sort of mental issue. Years later I found out that at this time she had a number of miscarriages. After the high school guy nearly killed me with his fists my mother, Helen, really started hitting me with a belt. Throughout my young life she had always hit me, but not Pat, with a belt. During this time, our family never celebrated birthdays and never took photos of the family children. I know that I have no photos of myself as an infant or as a child. In my twenties I began taking photos. As children, we only celebrated two Christmases. It was a brutal hungry life. The belt hitting went to a new higher level. She would chase after me in the back yard for some perceived infraction that I had committed. I never did anything bad in those days to her or her kids to warrant her beating me with a belt! She directed Pat, Don, Glen and Tim to chase after me in the backyard and hold me when they caught me. She would tell me, "if you run its only going to be worse when I catch you!" Helen then began to beat me with a brown electrical cord. The extreme intense pain of being whipped with an electrical cord would make me drop to the ground, writhing in intense pain. I could not understand why this was happening to me. It was at this time, that one afternoon, I was at my uncle Ray's home with his kids. We were playing in the street and as I ran into the street was hit by a WWII army jeep. I was hurt and nobody took me to the hospital! I could easily have been killed! We then moved to my uncle George and Sally's home. The beatings continued but not as severe because I was taller and bigger and I complained to my dad. Decades ago I forgave my mom for the beatings, as she had so many kids to deal with.

When I was at the Cactus Street home a number of profound events happened to me, but at the time, I did not understand. One event meeting a young girl named Kristen-I did understand. One of the strange X-files events that I experienced was when, on my way down to the Arkansas River mini falls, there was a Western store that had its merchandise related to horses and cows. When I was looking in the store, suddenly the number 50 kept popping into my mind. From then on, all my life, the number 50 has always been with me. Later in life I discovered that in the Egyptian Sun God

Ra beliefs, there was a 50-year time celebration called a jubilee. It would be 50 years from 1961 to 2001 when I would make a big scientific discovery. Some mysterious X-files entity, telling me of the importance of the number 50, was the sixth profound event that happened to me on Cactus Street.

As you can see, I experienced a pretty brutal life from 1960 to 1962 on Cactus Street in Pueblo, Colorado. My family was incredibly poor when we lived there. Later on in life, after I asked my mother, Helen, why we had suffered so much on Cactus Street, she told me that my father had past due bills to vendors such as Coors and The Walter Brewing Company. When my father's restaurant went broke in Rocky Ford he owed a lot of money to vendors. They had to pay off these bills because they were planning to go into the restaurant business in Colorado Springs. Already by 1961 and 1962 my dad's older brother, Joseph, had started a restaurant in Security, Colorado, south of Colorado Springs. In order to start a new restaurant business in Colorado Springs and get credit from vendors these bills had to be paid. All of the Masias children suffered because of these vendor bills. I remember a number of times when our small box refrigerator was empty and the children were so hungry that they were eating a raw onion. When we did have some groceries and fruit being even more rare, apples and oranges were always cut into quarters.

The tiny home on Cactus Street that we lived in for two years was very small. It had no city water, sewer or gas service. It had a cistern and electricity. There was a septic system. My folks used electric space heaters in the winter and the kitchen oven to warm the house. The winters were cold in this old drafty house. From 1960 to 1962 eight children and my folks lived in this tiny structure. The winters at this place were really bad. When you are cold and hungry in your home, and you are a young child with substandard shoes and clothes, it was very hard to be confident going to school and try to learn with the other kids, who had warm homes, plenty of groceries and nice clothes to wear. To compound the issue of our suffering, I, as the oldest son, was betrayed by a young boy, Bo, who claimed to be my friend. I almost died from a savage beating by a South High School brawler. I had experienced many brutal days on Cactus Street, and almost died there. However, I also experienced four astonishing events that would set the stage for the rest of my life and follow me into the universe.

On that beautiful day of May 18, 1962, when Mr. Smith introduced me to Kristen, it was an astonishing magical day that had opened up a whole new chapter in my life. I had liked a girl at Goodnight school, Cathy, but when I met my fate in Kristen my life took a total new direction. My thoughts were that Mr. Smith liked me so it was possible that I would see Kristen again. I was very happy for what the future would hold. But it was not to be for love would be lost again. At the end of May 1962, my parents told me we were moving back to our previous home and moving into my aunt and uncle's home on 15th street. I was going back to Catholic school. I was devastated by their news. I had just met Kristen and had experienced an amazing, positive, paranormal X-Files event. I knew that if I moved away, I would never see this girl again. For a brief moment in time, I saw another wonderful life that I did not know existed. I had briefly crossed through the Einstein-Rosen Bridge Stargate, so to speak, and my folks reached in and pulled me out when they said we were moving back to an old neighborhood. It was fate that it happened this way.

Then there was a reprieve of sorts. For a brief time of about a month, in September of 1962, I attended Pitts Junior high school and then the Masias family moved back to our previous neighborhood. This home, for the first time in our lives, was by far the nicest home the Masias family had ever lived in. It was located on 15th Street and belonged to my aunt and uncle, Sally and George Masias. George was an older brother to my dad and had been in the army in World War II. My dad told me that uncle George repaired Sherman tanks in Europe during the war. He also warned me never to ask any of my uncles about their experiences in World War II. My father said that they went to hell and saw terrible things and did not want to talk about the war. My understanding is that all of my uncles, Joseph, Ray, George and Jess served in the Armed Forces of the United States during World War II. All four of them survived the greatest disaster in human history without any physical injuries. However, they certainly did suffer from post traumatic stress disorder because of what they did and saw, according to my dad.

So it was the first week of October 1962 that our family of 8 children and 2 parents moved into the most beautiful home we had ever lived in. Over the years I have thought about these events and how they played out in my life. My siblings and I really suffered at the Cactus home in Pueblo. To me the term cactus always meant dry, desert, hot and drenched in sunshine. Yet, only one half mile away, there was a small waterfall in the life giving Arkansas River. The area where we lived was a metaphor for ancient Egypt: hot, dry, sunshine with the Nile River nearby - in this case the Arkansas River. In ancient Egypt there was Ra the Sun God, one of the top deities besides Isis and Osiris, in the pantheon of Egyptian gods. When I met Kristen she was like a Sun Goddess who came to rescue me from the rigors of the Cactus home, where I was almost killed, and guided me and my family to a beautiful home on 15th Street in Pueblo.

The home we moved into on October 1962 was bigger than any home we had ever lived in and it was beautiful, both inside and out. The main road into this community was paved and it passed right past our new home. Some of the homes next to us on 15th street were nice, like of those on Cherry Lane. The home sat on a lot maybe 60 feet wide and 100 feet long. It had a one car garage and grass in the front, back and side yards. The front and side of the property had a four foot tall, galvanized, chain link fence. A five-foot tall wood fence ran the distance of the back property line with the gate in the back yard. Two blocks south of our home was a new grocery store, big and modern for its time. Across the street, south and east, was an empty field that contained a small debris field maybe 20 feet by 20 feet of large white, sand stone blocks that someone had dumped in the field. When I first saw these limestone ruins, I was immediately interested in them because they reminded me of the fallen down temple debris of ancient Greece and Rome. Many times, I went over there to examine them and I found intricate carvings on the stone blocks which indicated to me professional stone masons had worked on the sandstone blocks. These sandstone ruins fit right into the stories my parents told me and the books they showed me about Egypt, Greece and Rome. The "discovery" of the ruins by me, next to my uncle George and Sally's home, was yet another event written in the stars. The two alien encounters I had as a little boy and the five profound events, including meeting Kristen at Goodnight school. All of these X-files events- were supposed to happen to me because of fate. These events and others would continue to follow me all my life and I would begin to understand them when I built my home in 1982 in Green Mountain Falls, Colorado.

The home on 15th street and the green grass and the garage was like a palace to me and my siblings. Living at the Cactus Street home was very difficult and brutal at times for me and my siblings. But it was fate and my destiny to live there because that's where I encountered the 6 profound events that have had, and continue to have, an effect on my life in scientific research and discoveries. I do not regret having lived there because I learned a great deal there and it set the stage for the rest of my life. I would not change what happened.

The inside of the new home was beautiful. It had wood floors, a nice modern kitchen and bath and there was beautiful varnished yellow 1 X 8 tongue and groove pine wood paneling on some of the walls. There were three bedrooms, living room, kitchen and bath upstairs. Downstairs, in the basement, there was a very large room, one bedroom and a gas utility room with a washer and a dryer next to the basement stairs. Me and my siblings had never seen such luxury at all the other small homes we lived in. We had a paved road next to the home, city water, central gas heat, electricity and city sewer service. I remember that all of the older siblings were very happy to be moving to this home. They knew and understood the suffering we were going through.

I am not positive, but my uncle George may have built this home with his own hands. I know as a fact, that my dad and uncle George built a back addition to this home that ran the length of the home. I know this because my dad took me there on numerous trips to help do the construction and cleanup. When I was 11, my dad and I built a new kitchen improvement to the Cactus home. We went to the lumberyard a number of times to buy the materials for the kitchen area. My first experiences with carpentry, that I can remember, was when I was attending Catholic school in the fourth grade and we lived in Mr Veller's home. This home was about one half mile from our new 15th Street home in 1959. My father showed me how to use a hand saw and a hammer to pound and drive nails into lumber. It was at the Veller's home that I first began to construct small toys and houses out of scrap 2 x 4's for me and my younger brothers. So in 1961, when I helped my dad build the kitchen improvements to the Cactus home, I was really happy with what my dad and I had accomplished in that kitchen. My father was happy with my natural carpenter abilities because he then bought me all the wood parts for my Golden Gate Bridge science project.

I learned a lot of carpenter skills in 1961 and 1962 from my dad and his brother George when I helped build George and Sally's home addition. So, when I finally found out that we were moving there, I was happy but still very upset because I felt that I would never see Kristen again. It was in October 1962 when my parents enrolled me again at the Sacred Heart Catholic school in Pueblo, Colorado. I was not happy about the prospect of going back to Catholic school, because I knew how rigid and mean the Catholic school system can be and were to me in the past. When I think back over the years and examine what happened, I can see patterns of behavior. I had to figure out the reasons for my parents' actions on my own because they were not forthcoming in talking about our family matters. Years later, I would find out that they did keep family secrets.

Pueblo in the fifties and sixties was plagued by gang violence and an ethnic social phenomenon called the Pachucos. I heard various people talk about these young Mexican-American gang members and their violent behavior. The 15th Street home was located in an economically and socially depressed area. Our immediate next door neighbors, the Gons, and surroundings did not have any gang affiliations that I ever saw. To this day, I believe that my parents sent me to Catholic school to keep me away from gang activity, which was good. But, as I said earlier, I knew we were very poor.

Going to Catholic school cost money and my folks had to pay some kind of tuition for me to attend. My mother told me that Father Sierra had made some sort of financial arrangements, on my behalf, so I could attend Sacred Heart Catholic School. My folks and I knew Father Sierra, as he was the presiding parish priest at the local church, which was one mile away from our 15th Street home. But I knew Father Sierra better as my school bus driver. Every day, Father Sierra would drive me and other Catholic school students, in a yellow bus, to Sacred Heart Catholic School, which was located north of downtown Pueblo. I remember that bus ride very well from October 1962 to June 1963. On the bus, with other peaceful Catholic school students, were two young, very tough and violent students. One guys name was Floyd, a young Mexican boy about 15 years old. His younger sister was in my class at Sacred Heart. Floyd's friend, Mike, was a white kid with sandy light-brown hair. Both of these tough teenagers were big and probably each weighed 150 pounds. They had a reputation for beating students up and I saw them take lunch money and punch students on the bus. These two toughs would be dropped off at a bus stop, two blocks from Freed Junior High School, where I believe they attended school. I never saw them at Sacred Heart School. These two young guys terrorized the school bus and I was constantly worried and on guard. Just one year before, while at the Cactus home, a South High School guy had savagely beaten and almost killed me with his fists. Father Sierra knew about these two alpha males who hurt people on the bus, but I never saw a resolution of the fear on this Catholic bus.

I attended Catholic school from October 1963 to June 1964. In October, I joined the school football team and played as a running back. We did not win any games. I was very lucky that I didn't get a permanent football injury. Even though I did not want to be at the school, I was required to attend Mass at 7 a.m. and then go to Catholic classes before 8 a.m., 5 days a week. Then on Saturday I had to return to Father Sierra's church and confess my sins to him in the confessional. Then I was required to return on Sunday for the High Mass. Then there were the various days when you had to abstain from meat and fasting was required. In addition, there were the various festival events, such as, the Stations of the Cross Observance, which was a required attendance. Boys had to dress in dress slacks and white shirts and the girls wore burgundy dresses and white blouses. I made the best of the situation I did not want to be in. One small element of this Catholic school, that made it better, was there were two Lay teachers, Mr. Quinn and Mr. Brady. Instead of being taught by nuns all day I had a couple of male teachers with sport clothes on and it felt better. This school was very small with maybe 150 students. I kept studying as hard as I could and I never caused any problems at home or school.

I never had a girlfriend, which was forbidden at school. The teen-age girl and her family, the Gons, who lived next door to us, never spoke to us once in the almost three years we lived on 15th street. I did average on my school work, which I think was good, because for years before and while going to Catholic school, we were still not getting proper nourishment. Finally, in 1963 or thereabouts, our family received brown boxes of cheese, peanut butter and salmon fish that were called food commodities. We were happy to have these government food staples. While at the Catholic school, I also joined the basketball team. I really enjoyed playing basketball in the nice new gymnasium. In football, I had scored some touchdowns, but it was brutal being slammed by guys who outweighed me by 50 pounds because I was under weight. In basketball I was more comfortable because I could run and dribble the ball much more effectively. I scored some good points and we won some games. At Sacred Heart I actually learned in school and that was when I took an interest in drawing and designing structures. Even at this time, I still read books on the Egyptians, Greeks and Romans, as I never lost my love for the ancient world and history.

One week, past the middle of November 1963, there was some sort of after school function that I was supposed to attend. My parents were driving an old beater automobile that broke down and my dad could not drive me there to school at night. The next morning at 7 o'clock a.m., in the cathedral church, just before mass began, the principal or boss of the school system, Monsignor Loss, suddenly appeared about 20 feet away from me in the church aisle. He was wearing his traditional black gown or frock, trimmed in maroon, next to the front thick fabric buttons. He began to shout at me and demanded to know why I had missed last night's function. His very violent verbal assault on me lasted for more than 5 minutes, because he made me get out of the church pew and squeeze past my other classmates to approach him in the middle of the cathedral. When I reached him in the middle of the cathedral he began his verbal attack on me. The Monsignor was about 6 feet tall and towered over me. I remember looking at my fellow male and female classmates faces. The girls were particularly upset by the verbal assault. I knew most of them and they liked me. A few days later at school, a student named Jim told me President Kennedy had been shot. A number of days after Monsignor Loss had verbally assaulted me in the cathedral, in front of my entire class, the only Catholic president in US history was assassinated in Dallas, Texas on November 22, 1963. Jim, the

Catholic student who told me about Kennedy being shot, was related to an auto sales company of Pueblo in 1963. The Catholic school community was devastated by this tragedy and the Christmas of 1963 was muted by sadness.

1964 came and my dad and I started driving to Manitou Springs, Colorado on the weekends on a regular basis. We were helping my uncle Joseph run his restaurant called the Mission Bell Inn. We had actually started driving to Manitou Springs in the spring of 1962 on a sporadic basis. My uncle George would lend us his new car to make the trips. In June of 1964 when I graduated from the eighth grade at Sacred Heart Catholic school, suddenly my parents pulled me out of Catholic school. That summer, we drove to the Mission Bell all the time for the summer tourist season to help my uncle Joseph.

At the same time, my folks enrolled me at Freed Junior High School in Pueblo. This school was, I believe, a couple of miles from the Colorado State Hospital. From September 1964 to December 1964 I attended Freed Junior High School. It was here that I was first exposed to the Elvis Presley and James Dean bad boys of the world. Unlike the guys at Sacred Heart, who were religious bookworms and not cool, there were cool James Dean types and yet not involved in gang activity. After school, I did not feel threatened like I did from the neighborhood I had lived in previously. Like Sacred Heart school I also learned some good subject matters. This Junior High was huge with hundreds of students but I adjusted pretty fast. At the time, I thought all my teachers were quite professional and cool compared to some of the mean religious people at Sacred Heart. I earned good grades at Freed Junior High School and I met two students that I still remember to this day.

My best guy friend at Freed was Bob. This guy was cool. He was quiet, yet he looked like a blonde Elvis with the same hairstyle and he was about six feet tall. He backed up his swagger but he was not mean. I had other male friends who were cool but none like Bob.

The second person who made an amazing impression on me was a young girl in several of my classes named Diana. We sat near each other in classes and she always smiled and said hello to me in the halls. Outside on the school grounds we sometimes talked. She was always nice to me and I never forgot about her. I had experienced incredible brutality; fist fights, a dog on fire, threats and almost being murdered - so when a beautiful young girl paid attention to me she made a big positive impact on me. Over the years, I have thought many times about Diana and how she fit into my life and legacy. For years, I had been studying the Greek and Roman myths of the gods and goddesses. If Diana had put on a Greek gown and kept her long blonde hair in her typical bun she would have walked into an ancient Greek temple and been the goddess Diana or Artemis. Artemis was the name of another female student I knew of at Freed. Diana or Artemis of the Greek pantheon of gods was a younger Greek goddess who was the twin sister of Apollo the Sun God. Later, at the end of my book, the reader will see that it was written in the stars, that Diana and I were fated to meet because of a possible fatal event that happened to me on the athletic field at Freed Junior High.

On a warm afternoon, at Freed, I was in my gym class running around the field with other students. To me it was a hot day with the Sun beating down on me. I began to feel sick to my stomach and my vision began to narrow as I began to faint on the field. Someone helped me to my feet and they walked me slowly with their arm and body against me, as they held me and we walked to the nurses office. This person said something about sunstroke. I felt so sick and it was difficult to walk but finally we arrived at the nurses office. The nurse was not there and my angel helped me to lay down on a canvas cot. I laid down and closed my eyes as I felt hot, flushed and dry. Someone gently put a wet cloth on my face and slowly caressed the cloth all over my face and top of my chest. I felt delirious and really ill. I felt a caring soft hand go across my forehead and heard a female voice give me words of encouragement. I opened my eyes briefly and I think I saw Diana. After all these years I cannot be 100% certain it was her because I was delirious. I believe that she was there when I had an almost fatal heart stroke event.

The personal connection between me and Diana transcended to ancient times and involves my scientific research and discovery. Diana was associated with the Sun God Apollo and was the moon God. In 1982, when I built my home and began to make my Ape-man, alien and Sun discoveries, there was a total lunar eclipse and a super moon event. To me this was an omen related to meeting Diana at Freed Junior High in Pueblo. This was my fate and it was written in the stars.

I was happy to leave the violence of Pueblo. Since 1962 when I was 12 years old, my father and sometimes my mother and one child, would drive to Manitou Springs to open my uncle Joseph's restaurant called the Mission Bell Inn on Crystal Park Road. It was open for business from 5 o'clock p.m. to 9 o'clock p.m., seven days a week. At first, our trips from Pueblo to Manitou Springs were sporadic but later we were going to work there all the time. My parents both told me in family meetings, just as they did years ago, that I as the oldest son, had a God given responsibility to set a good example and be a good oldest son like "in the Bible". I had to do this so that all the other younger brothers and sisters would follow my good example and work hard at the Mission Bell so we can make a living. If I did this and did not get into trouble with drugs, alcohol, girls or the police, me and the family would share in the wealth, good fortune and respect that the Mission Bell would bring our family.

Chapter 4 **COLORADO SPRINGS**

In the last years of 1963 - 1964 me and several Masias kids had attended Catholic school in Pueblo. I believed what my parents told me about working all together as a family and sharing in the fruits of our labor. I believed in the Bible and our patriarchal family. I had already been the good son in the Bible for twelve years. I made a covenant and gave a promise that I would set a good example and teach all the kids to work at the Mission Bell. We moved to 3605 West Pikes Peak Avenue in the winter of 1964. I was thoroughly committed to my parents and the Mission Bell Inn at this time.

I was attending West Junior High School when I met a young blonde girl named Kris who looked like Kristen in Pueblo. A little later on, I met Kris's brother Tim when I was attending Palmer high school. It had only been four months since I had met Diana at junior high in Pueblo. I became aware of, and later met Kris, in the spring of 1965 at West junior high school in Colorado Springs. It was really eerie how much Kris looked like Kristen. It wasn't until years later that I realized their facial similarities. I saw her at times in class and in the hallways at West junior. She would look at me in a submissive way with her blue eyes. I wanted to talk to her and I had asked her brother Tim about her. Tim, Kris and their parents started coming to the Mission Bell for dinner around 1966. Because of circumstances and my folks requiring me to work all of my spare time at the Mission Bell, I never was able to really talk to Kris. Kris' brother, Tim, and I continued to hang out together once in awhile until 1971 or 1972. In 1970 Tim's parents bought him a brand new 1970 Pontiac GTO and it was cool driving in that car with him. Then he and his family disappeared and they never came back to the Mission Bell. I drove by their home on several occasions and they still lived there. Then I began to hear about their family every Christmas starting in the early 70s. Local newspaper and television stations started doing stories when their family installed elaborate

Christmas decorations, including a manger, all over their home and yard. The huge Christmas celebration lights attracted people and cars from all over the city. These events went on every Christmas for about 10 years. Then the neighbors became mad and they stopped in the 1980s. Tim was on television in Pueblo where he was interviewed for the elaborate Christmas decorations on his home. Their family went all out to celebrate the birth of the Messiah.

Chapter 5   MANITOU SPRINGS

I continued going to school and working at the Mission Bell and teaching the seven children to work at the restaurant. It was at this home that a very serious event took place. About 5:30 a.m. one summer morning, I woke up to the smell of smoke. I quickly jumped out of bed to find the kitchen curtains on fire and the wall beginning to burn. I yelled and shouted out to my parents about a kitchen fire. My parents rushed to the kitchen and we found one of the kids hiding in the corner with matches. He was playing with matches and started the fire. I believe that I saved the entire Masias family from a tragic fire that day. It was at this time that my father beat up my mother in the kitchen for some reason. After a couple of years at this home and working at the Mission Bell, my sister Pat refused to work anymore in 1966. I continued to work at the Mission Bell and set a good example for all the other boys. I would go to school at 8 o'clock a.m. and get out of school at 3:15 p.m. I would rush home and take a shower and be at the Mission Bell by 4 o'clock p.m. We would open the doors at 5 o'clock p.m. and close at 9 o'clock p.m. After close and clean up, many times we did not get out until 11:30 p.m. I would then go home and do homework. I did this from 1964 to 1968 when I graduated from Manitou High, while living in Crystal Hills. My parents paid me $2 an hour and I would work 7 days a week. I was upset because they took out a lot of FICA and Social Security taxes from my checks. I never had much money left. I was told to share tips with both my parents and working brothers. I, as the oldest and strongest brother, was and did by far, expected to do the most work and I did before I graduated from Manitou high school. Many times I complained to my parents that I was working almost 50 hours a week in the busy summer time, sharing my tips with all the family members, and I was doing by far more work than all of them. I explained that I was not getting my share of the family wealth that they had promised me in 1962 and 1964. I remember my dad driving me in his brand new red Pontiac Star Chief down Pikes Peak and Colorado Avenue at 11:30

p.m. after the restaurant was closed. He was constantly giving me his lecture on being a good role model to all of the younger boys. He promised me that we would all share in the wealth. In 1964 we started making money at the Mission Bell. From 1964 to 2011the restaurant made millions of dollars. As the oldest son, working like crazy for my parents; my earliest labor laid the groundwork for them to make millions of dollars through the decades. My father was so rich he was a bank director! Being born into a patriarchal family I was told that, as the oldest son, as long as I was faithfully working and didn't get into trouble, someday I would be rewarded for my service with the Mission Bell.

One summer day in 1970, at the restaurant when Timothy was 13 years old and Sam was 12 years old, my dad let it slip that he had been giving $10,000 tax free gifts to all of these younger children except to Pat who had quit working at the Mission Bell in 1966. He said that he and my mother Helen had been doing this every year for years to avoid paying IRS taxes. It was and still is called a gift to family etc. I was 20 years old and had about $4,000 in savings. I was shocked stunned and very mad at my father and mother. I instantly realized that every Masias child from 7 years old to 18 years old had about $50,000 in each of their savings account! Most of the small Masias children had never worked at all and the oldest teenagers had not done or had the responsibilities that I had had. I had by far outworked all these young teenagers and they had $50,000 each and I had $4,000! At the same time, Tim had a girlfriend named Michelle and Sam had a girlfriend named Candy.

Both Tim and Sam began to rebel against our mother and father and started refusing to work at the Mission Bell. Tim got Michelle pregnant after three years. Tim was seventeen and Sam was sixteen and there had been constant fighting with them about not working at the Mission Bell. Then I was told that Sam's friend had demanded that Dan and Helen give him his $40,000. In 1970, when these two teenagers began to rebel and refused to work, me and Glen were forced to pick up the slack. Tim and Sam, by 1973, had literally stopped working. In 1971 to 1972 Glen was on the Manitou high school basketball team and involved with social activities at the school. He worked a light load at the Mission Bell. Don, in 1972, left for Boulder, Colorado with his fiance Debbie. They both attended the University of Colorado. Don paid for his pharmacy degree without any problem. Money was no object for him and Debbie because of my mom and dad. From 1970 - 1974 I was working harder than ever. It was at this time that my father began to literally lose his hair. It began to fall out and he became bald around 1972, because now his 10 year old daughter, Julie, began to rebel at school and at the Mission Bell.

At this time, from 1970 to 1974, Tim and Sam began to get involved in the things that teenagers do with their friends. Young teenagers all over America were doing the same things. I saw both him and Sam going to parties and woodsies with their friends up on Rampart Range Road. It was also at this time that 12 year old Julie began to really rebel. My father had to put my mother in the hospital for a nervous breakdown. By this time, Julie as well as Mark, had refused to work. Sam and Tim had each been given $40,000 savings accounts that they never earned. Julie, Mark, Sam, Tim and Don had all quit and Glen was part time. My dad, mom, Debbie, Ben, Glen and I, and a number of new employees that we had hired, began to run the Mission Bell. Despite all of the incredible teenage problems, I continued to be hopeful that my mom and dad would reward me with the money I had earned. At this time the Mission Bell and my parents were making money hand over fist. The restaurant made millions of dollars over the decades. My parents took trips to Las Vegas and bought new cars.

It was in 1973 that I met my future wife, Fawn, at the Mission Bell. Despite the huge amounts of money pouring into the Mission Bell my parents refused to pay me a decent wage. In 1974 I went to work for the Exchange National Bank in Colorado Springs. I applied for a civil service job with the federal government. I continued working off and on at the Mission Bell at night because I needed the money for bills. I continued to work at the Mission Bell, on a part-time, off and on basis, until the early 1980s. I had to work other job because my parents refused to honor the promises they had made with me in 1962 and 1964 in Pueblo, Colorado. I, as the oldest son, what supposed to set a good example for the younger children and teach them to work at the restaurant. I kept my promises to my parents to stay out of trouble and be a good role model and teach the younger kids to work at the Mission Bell. Sometime in the late 1980s my parents sold the restaurant to Glenn and Ben.

In 1973 I met Fawn, at the Mission Bell in Manitou Springs. We started dating and on August 21, 1976, Fawn and I were married at the Church in the Wildwood in Green Mountain Falls, Colorado. This non denominational church is located next to Hondo Avenue, the road that in 1982, I would build our home on - at the top of Hondo. Hondo is a Spanish word that means deep, low and profound. It was on Hondo, after I physically built our home, that from 1983 to 2016 that my scientific research discovered alien creatures and my infrared night vision camera took photos of mysterious Ape-Man creatures. As fate would have it, the name Hondo is also found at Roswell, New Mexico. The Hondo River is located near the famous UFO town of 1947. It was written in the stars that Roswell and my Hondo home would both be associated with aliens.

In 1974, when I met Fawn, she asked me to move into her home with her family and I did. Even though my folks had taken advantage of my labor and did not pay me what they promised, and because of my good saving habits, I was able to save up a good little nest egg. I had also worked two jobs at once and I did not pay rent at Fawns house so our finances were looking up.

In 1977 our son, Jeffrey Ryan was born. Fawn and I were joyful to welcome Jeffrey into our arms. We named him Ryan in honor of the star system Orion. We then moved to the Denver area in 1979. We were happy and optimistic because we had a beautiful baby boy. We had saved some money in the bank and we were happy about the future. Our family moved into the Bonsai Apartment complex one block south of Colfax Avenue near the Aurora city limits. While in the Denver area I did construction work and worked for Wendys, Taco Bueno, Taco Bell and 7-11.

Flashback

To Pueblo, Colorado, the steel and iron city; iron is a heavy element like gold and lead that are born in the cores of stars all over the universe. This well known scientific principle is at the heart of my scientific discovery about our Sun and the universe. It is 1962 and I am in the seventh grade at Sacred Heart Catholic School. One of the male students in my class is a little short white kid named John Wilson. He is a very diminutive looking kid and he is a very religious and devout Catholic. In my opinion, you cannot get any more devout than John Wilson was, unless you become a Catholic priest. Wilson was a symbol and exemplified complete faith and devotion to the Catholic faith. I knew him because I had classes with him.

Flashforward to the Bonsai Apartments of Denver, Colorado in June 1979. The apartment we lived in had a swimming pool and Fawn would take baby Jeff to the pool on hot days. She had become friends with a young mother named Pat who had two baby daughters who were Jeff's age. One evening in June 1979 at dusk, Fawn, Jeff and I were at poolside with Pat and her two daughters. Suddenly Pat said, "here comes my husband John! Now you can meet him." I looked over to see John about 100 feet away walking towards us. I immediately recognized the walk gait and silhouette of Pat's husband. It had been 18 years ago that I saw John Wilson at Sacred Heart Catholic school. Here he was walking out of the Denver sunset towards us. I was very surprised to see religious John Wilson walking towards me on that hot June night in Denver, Colorado. The minute he was within 50 feet of us I could see his face and hear his voice. I turned to his wife Pat and said, "I know your husband! I can't believe this!" I greeted John and shook his hand. I asked him if he remembered me from Sacred Heart. He said, "Yeah! I remember you from school and church!" All of us at the pool were blown away by the fact that John and I knew each other from 18 years ago in Pueblo, Colorado. We were all amazed by this fateful chance encounter and marveled at the odds of this happening with over 2 million people in Colorado.

When I think back over the years about my very rare chance encounter with John Wilson and his family, I came to realize that this event was related to all the other preordained paranormal events that have occurred in my life. I was a young Jewish boy who grew up in the sun drenched city of Pueblo. Pueblo was the backbone of the Industrial Revolution in the western United States. The Colorado Fuel and Iron Company sold metal products that came from the center of a giant exploding star billions of years ago. So here I was in the middle of the 20th century, a little kid growing up in Pueblo.

Some sort of fantastic, highly advanced, alien intelligence selected a little Jewish kid attending Sacred Heart Catholic school in 1963, in Pueblo, Colorado to reveal who they are. This responsibility was given to me, and part of this alien plan was put into play, when I met the religious John Wilson again in Denver in June 1979. In June 1981, Fawn, baby Jeff and I would say goodbye to John and Pat Wilson. We were returning to El Paso County to build our home on Hondo Avenue in Green Mountain Falls, Colorado. Within a year and a half of saying so long to the Wilson family in Denver we would be in our new home and staring at alien footprints in the snow! In my estimation, humans were created by an alien intelligence so advanced that they are probably the creators of the Big Bang and our universe! Their science is so advanced after billions of years, that it would appear to be magic to us.

Chapter 6 **DENVER**

In June of 1981, Fawn, baby Jeff and I loaded up an 18 foot UHaul truck with our belongings and moved back to Manitou Springs. We moved into a two bedroom cabin at the McLaughlin Lodge on Crystal Park Road. We moved to Manitou Springs across the street from my family's restaurant, the Mission Bell. Our family lived at this cabin for 3 or 4 months. We were extremely lucky to move into this cabin at the height of the tourist season. I knew Mr. Bickford at the McLaughlin Lodge and he was kind enough to let us move in. We lived at the lodge and then found out that our relatives, Jim and Joy Renzelman, were moving out of their small home on Duclo Avenue in Manitou Springs. They were moving to Texas and they offered us their really inexpensive home at $200 a month. In September of 1981, Fawn (who was pregnant with our daughter, Somer), baby Jeff and I moved to Duclo Avenue. Somer was born when we lived on Dulco. She was named in honor of the Summerians.

It was during this time that my mom and dad, Helen and Dan, signed over the title to the Hondo land to me. My parents had taken advantage of me for many years at the Mission Bell. When they signed over the title to this land to me I felt that they had partially redeemed their moral debt to me. I was very happy that day at the Bank of Manitou. I had already started putting home designs together for our Hondo building site in Green Mountain Falls. I was very excited about designing a new home for our growing family. Fawn was pregnant with baby Somer and I had every motivation and incentive to design and build our Hondo home. We had moved to Manitou Springs on June 1, 1981 and shortly thereafter, I had been up at our Hondo building site taking elevation measurements for our new home.

It was at the end of June 1981 that I contacted the Town Clerk of Green Mountain Falls and informed them that I wanted to build our home on Hondo Avenue. The town clerk handed me a few papers that describe the rules and regulations concerning home construction. I was required to attend a number of Green Mountain Falls council meetings of the town trustees to seek permission to build our home. I attended these required meetings and immediately ran into opposition from some council members and neighbors who did not want me to build my home they were skeptical and doubting.

Once I started construction on our home, I noticed that the Green Mountain Falls Marshal and his deputies were driving by my construction site all the time. There were only a few people living past my home so I thought it was odd that they drove by a lot. Later, I would find that this police behavior was no accident. I would hire an attorney to file a pending lawsuit against the Marshal and the town and I will be publishing a book about the marshal's office in Green Mountain Falls.

I finally received permission in a building permit in the fall of 1981 and immediately began construction. For the next six months, including a very cold winter, I diligently built our family home. Finally, I finished the home in the fall of 1982. I drew up the building plans for our home and physically dug the footers, after a front end loader removed a boulder from the site. Without any physical help from anyone, I framed up the entire home and closed it in from the weather. I poured the lower level concrete floor and ran all the electrical systems. My brother, Sam, hooked up the electrical panel. Auggie and I installed the plumbing system and I hung over 100 sheets of drywall. My wife, Fawn, helped me to finish the drywall texturing and I finished installing the cedar planks throughout the interior of our home. I physically built our home from the concrete footers to the roof line.

As fate would have it, in 1982 an incredible total lunar eclipse and super moon took place. The Sun, being the light source of this event, would also be the source of my scientific discoveries starting in 1982 when I built our home. It was written in the stars that in 1982 I would build the home, then through my research, I would make discoveries about highly advanced alien entities and our sun.

Chapter 7   **GREEN MTN. FALLS**

Our family moved into our home in the winter of 1982. We were in our home for the first week and at 11 p.m. there was suddenly a big pounding sound on the back of the house. I immediately turned on the back lights but did not see anything. My wife was very frightened by the loud pounding sound on the back. I stayed up for an hour and continued to look outside but nothing showed up. A month later, it had snowed 3 inches and I spotted human looking footprints in the snow on the side of our home. It was as though someone had floated down from the sky and taken off their socks. This entity then walked in an 8 foot half circle, leaving 8 inch long footprints, and then went back up into the sky! I was astonished by what I saw. I could not see footprints anyplace else and I was also puzzled. I was going to take photos of the footprints but was out of photo film. The next day it snowed and covered the prints. However, in the years ahead, I would see more footprints in the snow and I would take some good photos.

In the winter of 1984 we heard a somewhat loud thump on the roof, above the bathroom, at night. The next morning I went outside and looked at the roof. By this time, I was beginning to realize that some very strange, unnatural events were taking place at our home high up in the mountains. As I climbed the hill behind the house, I could see no footprints in the snow behind our home. When I looked at the roof, I saw what appeared to be simian footprints, hand prints and maybe the butt print of something that fell from four or five feet from the sky onto our roof!

See photo #1

An unknown alien landed on it's butt, on the roof and then walked around. Notice the 20 inch long flying plasma string aliens, on the right side of the roof, and the ghostly white plasma residue in the middle of the photo. These alien structures match photos and video taken from 2006 to 2016.

With the physical evidence of various simian footprints in the snow, on top of our roof, and the previous night hearing a muffled thud on the roof, I was now convinced that we were being visited by some sort of small unknown simian creatures! We were now on the lookout for the mysterious creature that was visiting our archaeology home site. The reason that I say archeology homesite is that an M shaped 50 ton boulder sits in my front yard. On the side, facing the road, there are mysterious pictographs on its flat, vertical wall. These symbols do resemble some of the ancient Dogon Sirius Sun-star symbols. The Dogon believe that highly advanced Star-Sun humanoid beings came to Earth in the distant past, and helped mankind to develop civilization. The very mysterious pictograph on my boulder, and the resemblance to the Dogon Sun-star symbols, in my mind, matches up with the discoveries I have made concerning our own Sun-Star. To me, it appears that there is a connection between the Sirius Sun-Star system and the Earth's Sun-Star solar system that involve some people in Africa, the pyramids and the Dogon people. There could also be other missing elements, but that remains to be seen, after more scientific research is done.

The winter of 1984 also saw a paranormal event take place out- side my daughter's bedroom window. My daughter, Somer, was 4 years old. That winter her cousin Kelly was visiting from Texas. The two noisy happy girls were in Somers bedroom. Suddenly, the girls started screaming. We rushed upstairs and Somer and Kelly both said a man was outside the bedroom window looking in at them. The bottom of the window is 12-feet above the ground. Both girls said that they saw the head of a man creature. Somer described the alien man as a light grey, white face with long sharp facial features. Somer and Kelly were the first to see the aliens who have been visiting our home site since 1982! When this frightening event took place in the winter of 1984 my wife and I now knew that very abnormal and strange events were taking place at our home. By now, we were both on the lookout for possible future sightings and told both our kids that there was nothing to fear. My wife and I never let our two kids out of our site both inside and outside of our home.

In the spring of 1985, my wife and I were in the backyard and I took a few photos of her with my Kodak Instamatic camera. When I took the photos I did not see anything unusual around Fawn. Everything seemed normal to me and her. Weeks later, when the photos were developed, one photo showed my wife surrounded in bursts of plasma energy above her head and a cascading flow of energy strings at her waist. When we first saw this photo we did not understand what the photo showed or what it meant.

See photo #2

This photo shows typical long strings of soft plasma energy

Years later, starting in 2006, my advanced infrared night vision cameras would start taking photos just like photo number 2 all the time. In the fall of 1986, I had taken photos in the backyard. When I did this I did not see anything unusual outside. When I had the photos developed, one photo showed a beautiful burgundy orb above a smaller white and burgundy orb below. Again, at the time, I did not understand what this photo meant. However, after 2006, my Advanced Tasco camera would take photos like this one in 1986. In the fall of 1988 I took some photos with our Olympus camera at night as an experiment.

See photo #3

Beautiful burgundy and white plasma orbs at top and bottom of photo

Three plasma orbs next to my tree, in the front yard

I knew that my Kodak camera had photographed mysterious phenomenon during the day. So I borrowed my sons Olympus camera and took photos at night. When I had the photos developed one photo showed three large orbs surrounding the tree in my front yard. With photo #3 I was now beginning to get a better idea of what was now happening around our home. Again, after 2006, my advanced night vision infrared cameras would start taking photos like photo # 3.

Then, on March 28, 1987, my son, Jeff, who was 11 years old, was playing with his friend Kevin. I was outside watching the boys play in the snow. Down the hill, in front of our home Jeff called to me and said, "Dad! There are strange footprints in the snow over here." I went down there and took a look. The boys playing down there had destroyed most of the snow prints. A couple were left and they did look like creature footprints I had seen before. That night I had an idea. I decided to stay up that night and watch the road to see if I could see anything. Around 11 p.m., as I watched from my lowest window from inside my home, suddenly I saw two small creatures running down the road... In front of my home. It was astounding to see too hairy ape like men running down the road! Immediately, I realized that these two phantoms were most likely the creatures responsible for the mystery footprints in the snow. About 8 seconds later, I saw two young girls and their large dog walk down the road right after the two creatures.

See photos #4 & #5

My son, Jeffs, hand next to alien footprint in 1/2 inch of snow

My son, Jeff's, hand next to smaller alien creatures footprint in 1/2 inch of snow.

The viewing conditions that night, outside of our home, was very good. The sky was covered with thin clouds and snow covered the ground. I think there must have been a full moon because I could clearly see the two running creatures. That night there was a lot of ambient light from the sky and the snow on the ground. Hours earlier, the snowplow truck had plowed the road and very cold ice crystals were slowly falling. Temperatures that night outside were bitter cold with one-half inch of crystal snow flakes covering the roadway. In photo #4 and #5 small rocks and pebbles can clearly be seen next to the alien footprints, the dog paw prints and the two girls moon boot footprints. As the alien creatures ran down the road and into my view from my lower level window, a remarkable event happened to the crystal snow on the roadway. As the warm blooded creatures ran over the bitter cold road their warm feet instantly "melted" the one half inch crystal snow. This astonishing event resulted in the exposure of the brown dirt of the road being exposed in the exact shape of the two alien creature footprints! Likewise, as the two neighbor girls and their dog walked down eight seconds after the creatures, their moon boots and dog paw prints left their images among the two alien creatures' footprints! Just like the warm blooded creatures bodies, the dog's paws also clearly left heat paw prints in the roadway, exposing the brown dirt of the road. The two young women were wearing boots that were very cold and did not allow heat out through the soles of the boots.

See photo #6

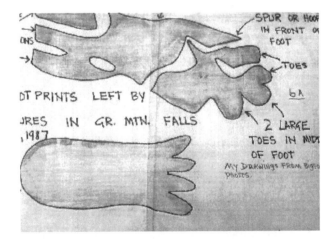

Authors drawing of 2 alien footprints, taken from 2 photographs

I did a very careful hand drawn depiction of the footprints of the two creatures. The larger humanoid alien creatures' footprints are quite unusual as the reader can see. The heel of the foot print has three digits sticking backwards. Maybe in another dimension or planet, it walks in another direction, as opposed to earth and its four dimensions. The smaller creatures' footprints looked remarkably like a human or chimpanzees footprint. As I described to a newspaper reporter in 1987, the two small creatures were not 8 foot tall Bigfoot creatures, but were five and maybe six foot tall. They were rather thin and hairy as they ran, their arms swung back and forth like a pendulum. They really looked like the little proto ape men in the movie 2001 a Space Odyssey.

In April of 1987, I went to the local newspaper, The Gazette Telegraph, and showed them photos of the alien footprints and told them about our mystery story. What followed were a series of newspaper stories. From 1987 to 1989 local newspapers all over Colorado and Denver wrote news stories about our alien creatures. Newspapers around the country also picked up our true Colorado story. At this time, I watched CNN do a story about Bigfoot. In 1988, NBC's Unsolved Mysteries contacted me. A segment director came out to our home and I provided him with alien creature hair. I obtained this hair when one of the creatures broke past a screen door at my neighbors cabin. The phantom was after fish left in the back porch. The hair was tested in California and it was determined to belong to an unknown primate. Because of the astonishing scientific DNA determination that the hair belonged to a real unknown creature, the Unsolved Mysteries people decided to do our story. The story was on national television in 1988 and was a big success. This story of ours has been on cable TV, in reruns for years. In 1989 Fate Magazine also did a story about our mysterious creatures. After all the news media reports in 1989 the excitement about the alien creatures calmed down. I continued to do my archaeological research, but my main focus was that I was building a new home. We continued to see mysterious footprints, on occasion, near our home.

On November 24th 1993 I thought I saw a flash of light outside. I took several photos in the direction of the flash and when I looked at the results one photo stood out.

See photo # 7

This photograph shows 3 alien faces in the upper right portion of photo. Another alien is to the left. When author took this photo, none of these aliens were there.

Photo #7 was taken by the Olympus camera. In the upper left hand quadrant of the photo there appears to be a white bear or pig laying on the ground. This mystery creature also looks like a Saint Bernard dog. On the upper right hand quadrant of the photo, there appears to be 3 alien faces! The first face, at the top of the photo, is large and white with a big black oval eye, small nose and mouth. This creature appears to be looking to the right. Right next to the large white alien face is the image of another unknown creature. The face of this creature looks like a Neanderthal caveman from Europe! It has a back sloping forehead, deep sub orbital large eye socket and a very large nose and a short chin. Just below this caveman creature is another alien face that is sitting at an angle on top of the Stonewall. This creature has a rounded top to its head with two large black oval eyes. The nose is barely perceptible but the open mouth is clearly visible. The creature appears to be looking at the camera! When I took photo #7, none of these creatures were visible to me. I saw a flash of light, so I began taking photos and this photograph is what turned up.

From 1990 to 2006 we did not see a lot of alien activity around our home. On occasions we saw footprints in the snow. In the winter and in the summer we saw prints in the mud. I have not put these photos in the book and have elected to put more important alien photos in the back of my book. On October 8, 1998 I took some photos with the Olympus camera at a site right near our home.

See photo #8

This photo shows a plasma orb, with a number of other smaller orbs.

Photograph #8 is very interesting to me because it is typical of many other infrared photos my night vision cameras would start photographing in 2006. My wife and I were at the site and I spotted an unusual looking small bird in this pine tree. I took a photo and the bird immediately flew away. When I had the photos developed, this photo shows an orb of plasma energy. When I took the photo we never saw this 3 foot wide plasma orb in front of us.

On December 18, 2001, right outside of our front door, I found a series of alien footprints in the snow. The night before fresh snow fell.

__See photo #9__

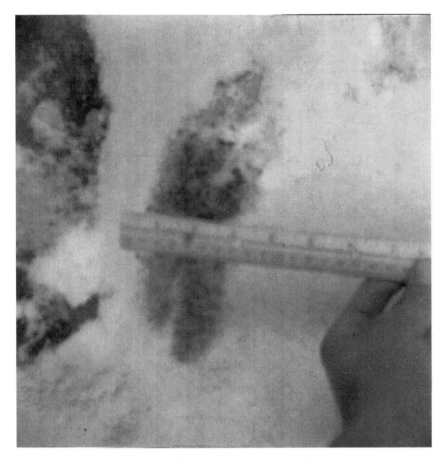

Photograph of an alien footprint near our front door.

Early on the morning of December 18, 2001 I walked out the front door to shovel snow. I saw alien footprints in the snow and went inside the house to get the Olympus camera. I could not find the camera, so I grabbed my old Kodak Instamatic and took photos of the footprints. A wood ruler indicates the width of the creature's foot. It somewhat resembles the large foot of the bigger creature I saw running in front of my house on March 28, 1987. The creature's foot has 2 large digits sticking backwards from its heel!

The Promised Land

My low tech cameras became high tech infrared night vision instruments. Before 2006 my best instruments for studying the alien creatures around my home was my instincts, finding footprints in the snow, watching and listening for sounds outside our home. When I did find signs of the creatures, I would photograph the evidence and make notes. In 2006 I purchased a Bushnell infrared night vision camera with motion sensing technology at the Walmart sporting goods department.

Almost immediately, my advanced infrared camera began taking photos of amazing and mysterious entities. At the time, I did not understand what they were. Years later, in 2016, I have a much better idea of what I have been dealing with. Over the years, I bought a number of books on the UFO and Bigfoot mysteries. They all had useful information that I recognized. By far the best book I bought on these subjects was a paperback book titled *UFO's A Manual for the Millennium* by Phil Cousineau. On page 104, I found information that is quite similar to the alien's that we have been photographing with my infrared cameras. This page describes how soft objects, such as nocturnal lights or orb like objects, transform into flying fireballs, UFO's and white humanoid alien entities. This is very close to what we have been experiencing at our archeological home site.

See Soft Objects UFO Manual by Phil Cousineau

UFO'S *A Manual for the Millennium*

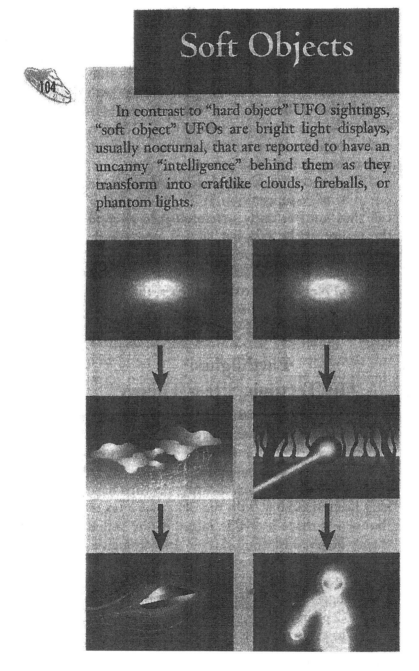

Soft Objects

In contrast to "hard object" UFO sightings, "soft object" UFOs are bright light displays, usually nocturnal, that are reported to have an uncanny "intelligence" behind them as they transform into craftlike clouds, fireballs, or phantom lights.

I have compiled a series of very advanced infrared night vision photos for the reader. These photos start with photo number 10. None of these photos have been photoshopped. A few of them have been flired, or given red and yellow highlights. This process exposes faint orbs that normally cannot be seen with the naked eye. Fliring is a very good scientific tool, to reveal hidden alien objects. See the faint objects in some of the photos.

Flashback to Nicholas Tesla in Colorado Springs, May 18, 1900

On May 18, 1900, Nicholas Tesla arrived by train in Colorado Springs. He is the world's greatest modern scientist, engineer, inventor and visionary, besides Albert Einstein. Without his scientific discoveries and development of those instruments, our modern world would be dark, cold, quiet and primitive. Our modern world of light, heat, fast transportation, flight, electronic communications, health care, entertainment, etc. would not be possible without the genius of Tesla being fulfilled in America. He lived in Colorado Springs for one year, and during that time, he conducted highly advanced scientific experiments at his laboratory. His research was so complicated, that nobody but Tesla knew exactly how his electronic instruments worked. While in Colorado Springs, he developed a mysterious instrument that he used to make contact with an alien intelligence. He told the news media that the aliens had given him a message. They gave Tesla a series of digits: 1, 2, 3. He added the three digits together, which totaled 6, and then multiplied that 6 by 3, which the aliens told him about. The total he came up with was 18. For the rest of his life, the number 3 ruled his life. Now back to 2016

What I am proposing, with great confidence, is that the aliens that Tesla contacted in 1900 are the same alien entities that my infrared cameras have taken thousands of photographs of. They are the same highly advanced humanoids of Tesla's day, who have expressed friendly gestures to me and my family – and allowed my infrared cameras to photograph them.

Most of photographs #10 to #28, show nocturnal orbs in the sky, thin flying beams of light and finally a bright alien humanoid with a photo of it's handprint in the snow. I will begin with the first infrared photograph #10.

Photo #10

This infrared photo shows the flying soft plasma strings that later turn into white alien humanoids as shown in the UFO Manual. Note the date. Location is our front yard.
A Uniden Infrared Night Vision System recorded these scenes.

Photo #11

Several large orbs with flying plasma string aliens in our front yard.
They object is a tree next to our home.

Photo #12

Beautiful infrared photo showing a soft alien humanoid, next to the tree in our front yard. This photo matches the UFO Manual information on aliens.

Photo #13

A bell shaped UFO landed in our front yard in this Wildview Camera Infrared photograph.

Photo #14

Fifteen different plasma orbs can be seen in this Bushnell Infrared photograph, taken next to our front yard tree. At the bottom of the tree the black tie strap holds a Tasco camera that has taken many alien photos.

Photo #15

WILDVIEW 08-20-2005 10:10:55

This stunning infrared photograph, taken next to our front yard tree, shows six soft flying plasma strings. They match the UFO Manual on alien appearances.

Photo #16

Twelve plasma orbs can be seen in this Infrared Bushnell photo taken on June 8, 2012

Photo #17

Seven plasma orbs can be seen in this Bushnell Infrared photo, taken on
August 30, 2012.

Photo #18

This beautiful infrared photo is the same photograph as photo #16. The photo has been flired to bring out hidden orbs.

Photo #19

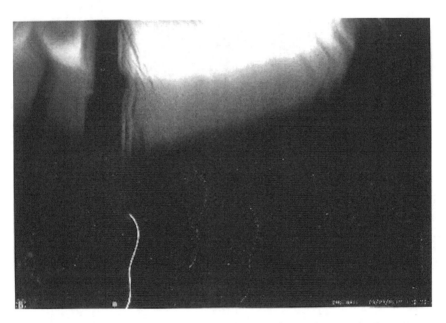

In the original infrared photograph, plasma orbs can be seen in the top left and center of this photo. Three flying plasma string aliens can be seen. The far left plasma string is highly energized. Our front yard tree is visible at the left.

Photo #20

Three flying plasma alien string creatures can be seen to the right of our front yard tree.

Photo #21

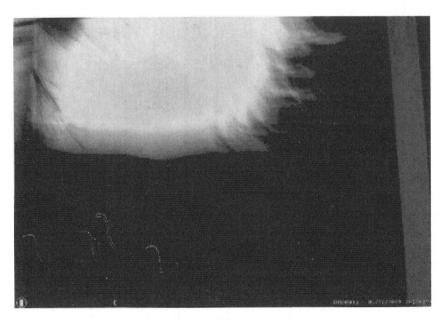

This beautiful lnfrared Bushnell photo shows five flying plasma alien creatures in our front yard. The photo has been flired to bring out hidden orbs. The giant orb at the top looks like our Sun.

Photo #22

My Tasco camera took a photo of a flying plasma alien string creature on June 9, 2014. It is very rare to photograph them during the day. The creature is at the back of the SUV.

Photo #23

This is an infrared photo of a highly advanced humanoid entity that, most likely, comes from our Sun. Note the point at the back of the head for communications.

Photo #24

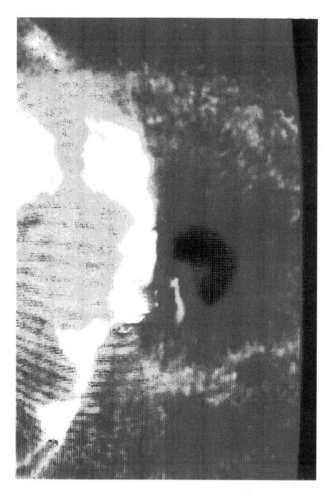

This photo was taken by a Japanese satellite studying the Sun. Infrared photo#23 and this photograph are identical. For this reason, and others, billion year old highly advanced Simian entities are living on the Sun..... and visiting the Earth. Thank you Dr. Hiro Shima.

Photo #25

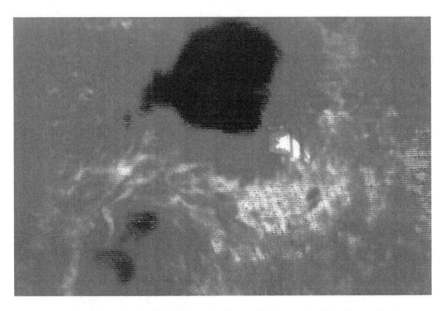

The same Japanese satelite that took photo 24 also took this photo of what they called a sun spot. It actually is a highly advanced entity. Notice it's strong resemblance to photo #23. Thank you Dr. Hiro Shima

Photo #26

10·06·2015 09:05:11 Ⓐ

This photo is an infrared night vision view that shows my Grand Cherokee and our Pine tree. Above my SUV are two orbs and behind it are nemerous orbs and flying plasma entities in our front yard.

Photo #27

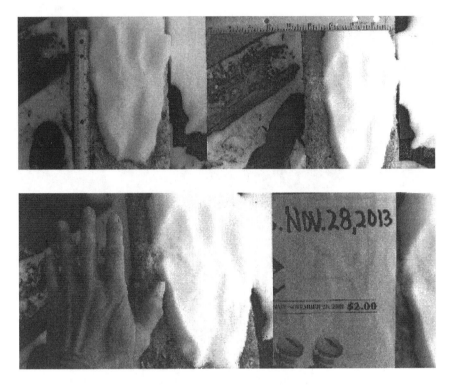

Highly advanced humanoid entity from the Sun left it's handprint in the snow, as a gesture of friendship to the Dan Masias family.

Photo #28

11·20·2015 10:37:17

Flying plasma entities in our front yard, next to our tree. Steps are visible to the left of huge boulder, which is behind the tree. Note the orb at the top next to the green box. The black circle in the middle of the photo is a Stargate that the aliens travel through. Every night I turn on my infrared night vision cameras, and the aliens appear on my flatscreen TV. Some nights there are hundreds of entities, while other nights there are just a few.

Stargate Discovered Worth Quintillions
$1,000,000,000,000,000,000

Discovery near Pikes Peak Colorado Springs - called 8th Wonder of the World.

By Ryan Anthony freelance science writer. - Colorado Springs, Manitou Springs, Green Mountain Falls, Colorado.

A science researcher says that he has discovered a Stargate on his archaeology property at the base of Pikes Peak. In 1982 Daniel Masias built his home in Green Mountain Falls and instantly noticed that X-Files events were taking place on his property. In 1988 he saw 2 small ape creatures running in front of his home. Masias said they looked just like the Ape Man creatures in the movie "2001- A Space Odyssey." In 1989 the story was on NBC's "Unsolved Mysteries."

Through the years many more X-Files events continued to occur and were recorded. In 2005 Daniel purchased high technology and infrared night vision cameras and pointed them at his property. The cameras started taking photos of alien creatures with large black eyes, Bigfoot, pictures of Moth Man, pictures of Ganesh the Hindu Elephant God, pictures of a werewolf, pictures of a Moai statue God from Easter Island, pictures of Anubis, Egyptian God of the Dead, pictures of a Chinese flying dragon or pterodactyl from the prehistoric era. The cameras have also taken photos of a flying and a landed dome shaped UFO, as well as a humanoid figure in his front yard that looks like Einstein, Abraham, or Moses. Daniel says that he has thousands of photos of never-before-seen alien creatures including 4 foot long string-like floating energy creatures like those described in "String Theory," the leading explanation by physicists to ex-

gate funds in America, individuals will band together to form new high-tech companies and businesses. The American economy will improve. He sees great scientific advances in high energy, plasma physics, fusion bio-transfer research, optical lensing, quantum physics, gravity and dark matter propulsion, dark energy synthesis, gravity optical lensing, electromagnetic bio-engineering, plasma biology, etc. He says that great strides will be made in biology, medicine, computers, energy generation, agriculture, transportation, climate technology etc. Masias said the Federal Government will build a new capital in Colorado Springs to meet alien ambassadors and visitors in the Stargate and to send off human scientific teams, explorers, colonizers and ambassadors, on trade, cultural and scientific delegations- to other civilizations in the Universe.

Asked about the history of the Stargate, Masias said it appears the existence of the Stargate was prophesied 1,600 years ago in 400 A.D. by the Roman Emperor Constantine. In 1961 a woman found and artifact in Western Colorado's Grand Mesa that shows Constantine's vision and discovery, at the base of Pikes Peak. The artifact appears to show all the various aspects of the Stargate as well as the 7 cities (mountains) of Cibola above Manitou Springs. The Stargate UFO is depicted in a blaze of energy above Pikes Peak. Father John Sierra the 45 year curator protector of the Constantine vision artifact, was Daniel Masias' friend, mentor and priest in Pueblo Colorado from 1958 to 1965. Source: Denver Post 6-20-2006- Independent Newspaper 6-29-2006.

Asked about the existence of aliens and the Stargate, Masias said he is in good company. President Carter and Regan, and astronauts Scott Carpenter, Ed Mitchell, Story

Epilogue I

(Buddha: The Sun, Moon, The Earth, The Truth cannot be hidden)

My name, Dan Masias, appears in the Oxford English Dictionary, On the Origin of English Words. These books are in libraries and cities all over the world. There are numerous epiphany and synchronicity events surrounding my name and my life. My infrared cameras have taken video and thousands of photographs of highly advanced alien entities. These entities are probably one or two billion years old, live on the Sun and are visiting the Earth on a daily basis. The Egyptians, Greeks, Romans, Incas as well as many other ancient civilizations worshiped the Sun as God. Some said that gold is the skin of the Gods.

The Sun was formed by a giant cloud of hydrogen gas that was created when a gigantic star exploded 4.8 billion years ago. Through the process of gravity causing rotation and eventually fusion, our hydrogen Sun was born, as well as, all the planets. Humans and most living organisms must have water to live. H2O or water consists of two atoms of hydrogen and one atom of oxygen. All humans are connected to hydrogen, the most abundant element in the universe. Today, scientists tell us that our bodies are literally made up of the elements of our sun and the stars. When a person takes a shower, drinks a cup of water, coffee or a soda, they are actually drinking the very chemical elements of our sun and the stars – in the Universe. You are tasting and swallowing the aftermath of the Big Bang.

The thousands of advanced videos and photographs that my cameras have taken, demonstrate that science does not truly understand the nature of life. Religion is in the same position. A few clues have been discovered deep in the oceans, where life has been discovered living on deadly toxic elements.....next to volcanic vents. It is counter intuitive to not believe that extremely advanced humanoid entities are living on our sun and visiting the Earth. My infrared photographs, and the Japanese Sun photographs, that match say this is true! Science tells us that without the Sun and the Moon, life as we know it would not exist on Earth. Science does not really understand the proton, neutron and hydrogen gas.

Epilogue

Likewise, because mankind has no idea that extremely advanced "God-Like" entities live on the Sun, man does not truly understand nature. There's no doubt that these entities have, over a couple billion years, "engineered" the Earth's physical environment. We know this environment as nature and specifically clouds. The water from clouds, combined with solar energy, has given rise to life on the Earth through photosynthesis and other processes. The Webster's Dictionary describes clouds as "A visible expanse of suspended droplets of water or ice particles in the air." Because of the highly advanced entities' scientific work on Earth for the last two billion years.....clouds are really floating *geometric crystalline*; highly advanced entities. These ghostly hydrogen gas *cities of the skies* are directly related to the Sun. Their waste products of crystal snow and water have given rise to life as we know it on Earth. this process has allowed human life to thrive, but roadblocks and firewalls have also been placed on manind's knowledge. One of these restictions has been demonstrated when Albert Einstein failed to discover the Unified Field Theory.

Acknowledgements

I would like to thank all the people who have spoken to me, over the years, concerning the subjects in my book. Thank you Phil Cousineau, for your insightful book UFO's Manual For the Millennium. Thank you Nicholas tesla, for your contact with the aliens in the Pikes Peak region in 1900. Thank you Albert Einstein for carefully calculating the sunflower orbit of Mercury around the Sun....which, in turn, led to your discovery of E=MC2 and changed the world for the better. And finally, thank you Albert for looking just like my Father Dan; we have a common Jewish ancestry. Thank you Apollo and your son Aesculapius The Healer. Thank you Descartes for saying God can be found in geometry. Thank you Astronaut Edgar Mitchell for saying aliens exist. Thank you President Ronald Reagan for your speech to the U.N. informing world members that an alien presence is among mankind.

Bibliography III

Cousineau, Phil. UFO's Manual for the Millennium. Harper Collins west, New York. 1995

Oxford English Dictionary
Oxford England. The Origin of English Words

Buddha Quote

The Hinode Japanese Sun Satellite

I published this book in 2003. The book is about scientific predictions, **based on volcanic regions of the Earth, that involve past and future events. The book turned out to be accurate. I have three more books coming out:** *The Man Who Walked out of the Pages of History II, Daniel Masias and GMF Police, and SOL.*

Printed in the United States
By Bookmasters